THE TRANSITION OF BECOMING

"We don't become when we arrive, we are constantly becoming as we arrive."

WARREN HAWKINS III

Thank you Jean for your support
— Warren Hawkins III

Thank you Jean
for your support
— Mayor Moirett(?)

Contents

Acknowledgments	vii
The Explanation	xiii
1. The Transition of: A Menace to Minister	1
2. The Transition of: Redemption	11
3. The Transition of: Embracing	23
Disclaimer	33
4. The Transition of: Realization	34
5. The Transition of: Being Sure vs Being Unsure	47
6. The Transition of: Redirection	61
7. The Transition of: Stride	74
8. The Transition of: Patient Expectation	84
9. The Transition of: Heart Alignment	95
10. The Transition of: Starting from the Bottom	104
11. The Transition of: Pressing	114
12. The Transition of: The Dark Room	120
13. The Transition of: Preparation	129
14. The Transition of: Multipurposed Responsibility	138
15. The Transition of: The Dry Valley	149
16. The Transition of: Promise Keeping	160
Recommended Reads	167
About the Author	169
Notes	171

Copyright © 2020 by Warren Hawkins III

All rights reserved. This book or any portion thereof may not be reproduced or used in any manner whatsoever.

Printed in the United States of America

First Printing, 2020

ISBN 978-1-7338442-2-2

Cover design by Anthony Rundles Jr., A. Rundles Design | IWILLNOTFAIL™
arundlesdesign.com

Editing by Shirley Fedorak, shirley.fedorak5@gmail.com

Author photograph by Ghost Hallmon, NEITH@ghosthallmon ghost@neith.co

Unless otherwise indicated, Scriptures are taken from:

The HOLY BIBLE: New International Version. (1973, 1978, 1984). International Bible Society.

KJV. (1979, 1980, 1982). King James Version. Cambridge, UK. Cambridge University Press.

NKJV. (1979, 1980, 1982). New King James Version. Nashville, Tennessee: Thomson Nelson Inc.

NLT. (1996). Holy Bible, New Living Translation. Wheaton, IL: Tyndale House Publishers, Inc. Used by permission. All rights reserved.

ESV: Study Bible : English Standard Version. Wheaton, Ill: Crossway Bibles, 2007. Print.

This book is dedicated specifically to this generation. We live in a day and age where so many of us are taking the brush out of society's hand and painting our own paths with what we deem as opportunity and success. But we have to realize that masterpieces take time. This generation is filled with so many people who want to become. I wrote this book to be a reminder for us all that in order to become, we have to first start by becoming. Our becoming is the transitioning bridge that connects who we are now with who we are meant to one day become. These words are a reminder that the only thing more important than who we will become tomorrow is who we are becoming today.

Acknowledgments

I first want to thank the Lord for all He has done in my becoming. Lord, thank you for the path You have painted for me on the canvas of my becoming. Thank you, Father, for aligning every piece that makes up the puzzle of who I am becoming each day. Lord, thank you for allowing me the opportunity to even become. Lord, I may not always appreciate or understand every experience, but I thank you for allowing each moment to shape and mold the path You have for my life. Lord, thank you for building and growing me. I thank you for truly taking Your time with me and allowing me to transition through experiences and seasons that allowed me to pick up the pieces of who I am meant to become along the way to my becoming. Lord, I thank you for Your unmerited grace and Your undeserved hand over my life. There are moments when I second guess and hope for other options, but Lord I thank you for still choosing me. Father, every page of my becoming has not been easy, but because I have You, I know this story was meant to be told.

I would also like to thank my dear mother of five. When I feel weak and hopeless, you are my spiritual backbone and my verbal defibrillator who zaps my belief and hope back into the rhythm of God's promises for my life. In moments when I have difficulty breathing my future into existence, your words are like an oxygen pump that helps me inhale a fresh breath to believe once again. Thank you for pointing out the mountain top for my life. Because of you, I am reminded to dream big. You remind me that the mountain top is attainable and achievable. You remind me that if I reach the mountain top God has for my life, it will help so many others have a clear view for their lives. I thank you, my mother of five, for also taking my hand and leading me down the path of my becoming. When I fall your hand stretches out to pick me back up. Your words are like footprints to guide my trail and our countless conversations are like a road sign to direct me down the right path. I believe in my becoming simply because you tell me I will one day become. I love you momma!

Next, I would like to thank my father. Dad, thank you for your patience and support in not only my becoming as a spiritual leader but as a man. I am forever grateful for your support and guidance. You not only hold me accountable for my decisions, but you are there like a stop sign to halt me in my tracks whenever there's a dead end ahead. Father, thank you for your calm, cool, and collected guidance. You are the calm in the storm. You remind me to think rationally, critically, and logically in all that I do. I also thank you, father, for not only supporting my becoming but believing in it. I remember after publishing my first book, *Shaped for Greater Works*, how you became my number one salesman. You purchased bulk copies of my book and everywhere you went you encouraged your coworkers, colleagues at the barbershop, and family friends to support my book. As a result of your efforts, I met so many individuals who were empowered by the message the Lord spoke through that book. Your efforts are truly monumental for me.

A special thank you to all of my siblings. To my brothers and my sister, I love each of you dearly. To my brothers, I am your keeper as each of you are mine. I thank each of you for being my backbone, extra set of lenses, and my shoulder to lean on. To my one and only sister, I truly cherish you. As your big brother, I am your captain and the one who is commissioned to guard and protect the throne of your becoming. I love you little sis! Thank you to my extended family. To my cousins, aunts, uncles, and grandparents, thank you for the prayers, the phone calls, and the nurture and support. Each of you are a piece to the puzzle of my becoming.

A special thank you to my hometown pastor, Dr. Douglas Petty. You are like a stop light in the road of my becoming as you remind me when it is necessary to pursue a certain path, to slow down and be cautious of my surroundings, and to sit in total stillness and wait on the green light of the Lord. Thank you for investing your time, leadership, and wisdom in me. This book is a return on what you have invested in me.

Next, I would like to thank those people whose helping hands play a role in my becoming. First, I would like to thank my dear friend, mentor, and fraternity brother, Cafabian Heard. I believe the Lord allowed you to divinely transition into my life. I believe God transitioned us into each other's lives so that we could help one another become. I believe you are like an aircraft marshal for my life. Whenever I am trying to land a vision or dream God put in my life, you are right there signaling and directing me to a perfect landing. I remember a day when I felt defeated and became discouraged. Instead of throwing a stone, you placed your hand on my shoulder and prayed healing and guidance over my life. Thank you, Fabe!

Next, I would like to thank my dear friend and fraternity brother Ghost Hallmon. I am forever grateful for you and the gift God has embedded within you. I thank you because you have played a huge role in my becoming. Every vision I have, you bring it to clear sight, and every time I conjure a plan you turn it into a masterplan. Working with you on creative content allows me to tap into a side of myself I never knew existed. Your creative vision not only challenges me but pushes me to awaken a piece of who I am. You taught me the importance of capturing the minds and hearts of people through creative content and visuals. Because of you, I will forever know that it is okay to be creative, unique, and innovative. Your creative eye is truly anointed, and I thank the Lord that our creativity met in order to create new ideas that will benefit this generation.

Next, I would like to thank my college best friend, Dynecia (Dee) Clark. I thank the Lord to have someone like you whose loyalty supersedes expectations. I thank the Lord that I have a friend who is also a helping hand in my becoming. You not only support me but you believe in me. You don't critique me, but you construct me and it is always genuine. There are times when I am lifting and balancing a lot, but you are always there to help lighten the burden. Instead of watching me struggle, you volunteer your services to help me carry the load. You remind me that my sight is foresight. Anytime I need your help you are always there. Anytime I need a listening ear, you are always there to hear. Not only do you believe in my vision, but you are always there to help me execute my vision. You are not just a friend but a lifelong partner in crime as we work toward stealing souls for the Kingdom of God. Dee, I thank you! This is only the beginning!

A special thank you to my fraternity brothers. I would like to thank the men of Alpha Phi Alpha Fraternity Incorporated. I thank each of you not only for brotherhood but for the daily dose of inspirational accountability. As a man of Alpha Phi Alpha Fraternity Inc., I stand on the backs of giants who refuse to lay down to systematic forms of oppression, discrimination, and social classism. I walk in the footprints of men who commissioned their lives for the morality of humanity and have forever left their imprint in the soil of this world through ministry, education, politics, and service. Because of you, in moments when I feel like abandoning the path, I look left and right and know the only way is onward and upward and never backwards.

Lastly, I would like to thank my graduate school colleagues. I thank each of you for inspiring me academically. Being engulfed in academic environments with each of you has truly propelled my intellectual and theological capabilities. I thank each of you for being a reflection of what I need to see. I am grateful for the opportunity to be sharpened by other intellectual minds and to have my lenses polished by the clear visions you behold. Each of you is forever embedded in my becoming. I publish my second book as a graduating advance standing one-year master's student of Clark Atlanta University.

The Explanation

Sometimes God will only show us the mountain top, but we have to trust the path along the way, and sometimes God will only show us the trail, but we must have faith that it will lead to the mountain top. In essence, the mountain top is who we are meant to be, what we can potentially achieve, and everything we are predestined to become. The trail up the mountain is a series of transitions that include different paths we must take and obstacles we must face in order to reach our destination. I assure you, we are not meant to just glare at our mountain top from afar. Regardless of who we are, there is a mountain top or high points we are meant to reach in our lives. The emphasis in this book is not solely on who we become once we arrive, but also on the essence of who we are potentially becoming on the path to this mountain top.

As I continue on the path to my mountain top, I am writing my second book as a 23-year old graduate master's level college student. I am enrolled in an accelerated curriculum program while also counter-balancing an overload of courses, an internship at a crisis shelter, and serving as a youth minister of a church. Despite all these opportunities, I became frustrated because I felt my becoming was not coming fast enough. My focus was not on who I currently was in that moment of my life as I wrote this book, but who I am meant to become. Sometimes the biggest challenge is not believing we are destined for greatness but believing in ourselves enough to endure the necessary processes that qualify us for the level of greatness we dream of.

As I sat in my office, I stared vaguely into the computer screen. While clicking through internet tabs, my mind continued to day dream. The more I day dreamed, the more I questioned the relevance of where I currently was in life. I began a subconscious wrestling match against my own thoughts. I felt as if I did not have the upper hand. I felt pinned down to the thought that everything I was experiencing was in vain and was not nourishing rain meant to sprout and blossom my future into existence. I envisioned the mountain top, my future, like a star that when I looked up seemed so close. Yet when I reached out, it seemed so far away. I became discouraged by my current path even though I believed this path to my master's degree, internship, and youth minister position were all essential in the process of my becoming. I was in a contradictory battle trying to find the balance between my see-saw emotions. I began to drown in doubt and sink to the deepest level of hopelessness.

In that moment of despair, my cell phone suddenly rang. I snapped out of my visualization of drowning in an ocean of my thoughts and picked up the phone. My mother was calling. Her timing could not have been more perfect. In that moment of feeling like I was about to drown in hopelessness, her phone call was like a rescue lifebuoy that would help guide me back to the shore of hopefulness. Instead of greeting her with a hello, I immediately started to tell her how I was feeling. I confessed that I was beginning to doubt the value of where I was in life. She encouraged me and explained how everything I was experiencing was shaping, molding, and propelling me for the work God has called me to do and who He has predestined me to become. She assured me that this constant change in transition and new seasons of my life was ultimately the best thing for me. Her next few words served as the capstone of our conversation. She said, "Son, in order to one day become, you must first start by becoming. And in order to become we have to transition. We become only by transition and with each transition you are becoming." She then said, "Son it's *The Transition of Becoming.*"

In that moment, it was like a light bulb suddenly appeared above my head. Little did I know that I would inhale these words as an idea for the next book I would exhale into this world. I had a sudden moment of epiphany, and I was struck with a life-changing realization. These words were essential to summarizing my process. They helped everything I had experienced in the past few months make sense. *The Transition of Becoming* is more than just a book title; these words will serve as a lifelong reference for my journey. These words are uniquely profound to who I currently am, who I am becoming, and who I am transitioning to one day become. In that moment I realized that the visions, aspirations, and dreams the Lord placed in my heart are meant to become. But in order for those things to become, I had to start by becoming.

Transition means the progression, passing, and development of something. Becoming means the process of coming to be something or of passing into a state.[1] Therefore, the greatness in your mind and that you aspire to be, already exists. You are just in the transition of becoming it. The very idea that replays repeatedly through the screen of your imagination already exists, you are just in the transition of it becoming reality. The very life you picture for yourself is already yours, you are just in the transition of that life becoming yours. Understand, that only by transition do we go from potentiality to actuality.

I wrote this book so that we do not just bask in the idea of potentiality, but so that we walk into the actuality of who we are meant to become. We must go through the process of transition in order to move from potentiality to actuality. Consequently, we can feel like we are being punished when we are really being molded. Perhaps we may feel like we are being buried, but we're really being planted. Sometimes we feel like we are being disturbed when we are simply being developed. Often we can feel like we are being deterred from our destination when we are really being redirected down a new path. We may think we are in a storm when it is really just a cleansing. Sometimes we feel like we're being hidden when God is really covering us. Sometimes we feel like we're being held captive when in actuality God is molding us in the womb of closed curtains and closed doors so that we won't come out prematurely. It is only by the transition, which is the change and movement in our lives, that we truly move toward who we are meant to become.

The process of transition gets real for me as well. I, too, have moments packed with ambiguity and uncertainty. There are times when I feel like I am in a fight between the ideal of me either operating in my sight or my foresight. I am learning to keep my eyes open to what's in front of me while still taking the time to close my eyes and visualize what is ahead. I am learning to endure the now while also embracing the future. I am learning to be patient in my becoming because sometimes it takes time for us to become. Therefore, I wrote this book for anyone who has a dream that stirs their consciousness. I wrote this for anyone who knows there is something great deep down inside of them that is not meant to be digested by their mere imagination but meant to be manifested into realization. I wrote this book for anyone who knows they are meant to become. I wrote this book for anyone who may think their time has passed. I wrote this book for anyone who goes to bed at night with an alarming passion that wakes them in the morning. I wrote this book to remind you that it is okay to dream big, and that you do not have to dream small. I wrote this book to remind you that the vision, dream, and desire to achieve within you is not a mere coincidence but an act of God's divine intent. I also wrote this book to inform you that greatness is not exclusive. Achieving greatness and living out the dreams God has for your life is not only for a certain group of people. You, too, can become what you see and what you believe.

Sometimes we can find ourselves in a position similar to two cliffs separated by a deep ravine. As you stand on the edge of one cliff, a great gulf separates you from the other side of where you want to be in life. You can't help but think fondly of this other side, because the other side beholds everything you want to become in this life. You want to step toward the other side, but there is an invisible path that can be quite intimidating. In the same essence, transition is the invisible path that can be quiet intimidating, discouraging, and confusing. Throughout this book, you will discover that sometimes God does not pick us up and take us to the other side of who we are meant to become. We have to take the step and trust that God's hand will be the bridge that guides us as we transition to the other side. God never promised it would be easy, nor that it would happen overnight. **Habakkuk 2:3 |NLT|** *"For still the vision awaits its appointed time; it hastens to the end—it will not lie. If it seems slow, wait for it; it will surely come; it will not delay."*

I am intentionally writing this explanation during my transition of who I am becoming so that each of us can know we do not become when we arrive, we are constantly becoming as we arrive. I wrote this book for us, as our own personal journal or diary. One day, this book shall serve as our testimonial bookmark to help others with their stories. We shall flip back to these pages of our lives and come to realize the reason we've become is because we have endured and experienced through transition. That's the true fragrance of this book that I hope you inhale, as you exhale a manifestation into this world of not only believing but also becoming who you are meant to be. I write this book not as someone who is looking back and stretching out my hand after reaching the mountain top, but also someone who is asking for you to walk with me as we transition toward the mountain top together. One day when we finally become, we will be able to look back, and maybe even laugh, cry, and reflect, but most importantly, we will be able to use our transitions as a road sign to show others that we didn't become after we arrived, but we were constantly becoming as we were arriving.

There's no such thing as steps or instructions to our becoming. But there is such a thing as transitioning in order to become. Every new path, moment, decision, and experience is its own transition and a piece to the puzzle that completes our becoming. That's the case with this very book you are reading now. Each moment, experience, and chapter is its very own transition. And every transition has its own path and learning experience that will help us understand, appreciate, and trust the process of our becoming.

You are about to embark on a path to the mountain top of your destiny. A path that is filled with a series of tears, closed doors, and No's. But a path also filled with opportunity, lessons, growth, maturity, and redirection. And remember, we don't become when we arrive, we are constantly becoming as we arrive. See you at the end.

1

The Transition of: A Menace to Minister
LETTER TO YOUNGER SELF

A menace is a person or thing that is likely to cause harm. It may be a threat or danger[1].

If I could say anything to my younger self I would say that a gift you're not purposed for is packaged in the form of a trap, and a path that is not meant to be taken can lead to a dead end. I would also tell my younger self that a burning passion for the wrong match can light a path of destruction and choosing the wrong destination can be the direction of a lost soul.

Dear younger self, I hope you find this letter as it is intended to save us both from a battle that we no longer have to fight, and to prescribe a treatment for a wound that you can heal so that I no longer feel its pain. I hope this letter serves as a warning sign of what lies ahead. This letter shall remove the scales from the eyes of my younger self and provide us with the foresight to embrace our path of transition. If only you knew what I know now, I would not find myself fighting a battle and unwrapping a wound that was covered but never treated. Because you could not picture our life without what we once loved, I now live with the thermal burns of the fire that we never extinguished within.

This fire, wound, and battle that I speak of derives from the menace that lingers inside of who you are today. You, as my younger self, are the menace. You are the fire left unextinguished, the wound left untreated, and the fight I find myself battling. At times, I find the menace I once was trespasses in my consciousness and declares an emotional war on the minister I've become. The menace that I once was on the path of becoming intersects with the transition of who I am meant to become.

Truthfully, we have not wholeheartedly forgiven ourselves for not becoming what we thought we were supposed to become. I still have not let go of the fact that who I am currently becoming is not what you wanted to become. When we were younger, we aspired to be a professional NBA basketball player, which pulled us toward a different path of becoming. I refer to you as a menace because, by definition, menace means a person or thing that is likely to cause harm, and that can be a threat or danger.

The path we once thought we were supposed to take was actually harming who God ultimately called us to become. What we initially wanted to become and accomplish in this life was not God's plan for our life. As stated, *a gift you're not purposed for is packaged in the form of a trap, and a path that is not meant to be taken can lead to a dead end. Having a burning passion for the wrong match can light a path of destruction and choosing the wrong destination can be the direction of a lost soul.*

Basketball was the gift that we possessed. However, just because we possessed this gift does not mean we were predestined to unwrap it as our life's path and purpose. The burning passion we once possessed for this sport was like lit matches that would have ultimately burned who God truly meant for me to become. And us choosing the road of wanting to become a professional NBA basketball player was actually a direction that would lead us to a lost life of unfulfilled purpose. It would have led us down a road of nothingness. Therefore, basketball is our menace. Basketball is the very thing that posed a threat to the purpose and call God had for us to preach His Gospel. Unfortunately, as I continue my transition of becoming, at times I find myself still conflicted with who you once were and who I am currently transitioning to be. I still find myself struggling with digesting the undeniable notion that our becoming has taken the path of me now being a minister of the Gospel and being called to preach and proclaim the word of God.

Likewise, many of us have a menace inside of us that contends with who we are becoming today. Our menace can be the very thing that posed a threat and harm to our life. I am asking you to forgive yourself for not becoming what you wanted to be because maybe what you wanted to become could have been the very menace that led you to a path of harm and destruction. What if the very gift you wanted to unwrap would actually lead to a trap because it was not packaged in who you were meant to become? What if the very road you once wanted to take would have led you to a path that was unfulfilling and purposeless, and was actually a dead end? What if the very thing you had a burning passion for would have burned to ashes your true life's destiny and who you were truly meant to become? What if the very destination you predetermined for your life was the direction that would have led you to a life of feeling lost? What is in your life that is your menace? What hasn't your younger self let go of? What was it that you wanted to become but didn't? What have you not forgiven yourself for not becoming?

You may still have remnants of menace inside of who you are. Likewise, many of us still have pieces of who we wanted to become inside of who we are currently becoming. Many of us have a menace that is in the form of our younger selves. I want you to confront your menace because if you don't, it has the potential to harm who you are becoming today and who you are meant to become in the future. The menace inside of us places scales over our eyes that blind us from the true path we are meant to take for our lives. If we do not extinguish the burning flames of our menace within, it can burn the path God wants us to take and who He has called us to be. Understand that letting go of our menace may not happen overnight. Therefore, I ask you, what is your menace? Your menace can be in the form of a relationship that didn't work out that you may still be longing for. Your menace can be a job, position, or promotion that you hoped to achieve but didn't receive. Your menace can be something you aspired to be but you weren't able to become. Again, I ask, what is your menace?

Now as a minister, I am still in the becoming of conquering the menace that lies dormant within us. Although we have said Yes to our calling and our life's purpose of preaching the Gospel, our predetermined plans did not extinguish overnight. When we said Yes to God, it became an ongoing daily sacrifice of our own heart's desires. When we said, "I do," to the Lord's plans for our life, it became vows that we could not take back. There are moments when I question if you were ready to say "I do" to the calling the Lord placed on our life. Because of you, there are moments when I have thoughts of divorcing myself from what we vowed. I often find myself on my knees and renewing our vows with the Lord through prayer and reminding myself that through thick and thin we promised to stay the course. But now I am the bearer of the scars that you caused from not letting go of the sport we once loved.

Sometimes I feel a sense of denial I must subconsciously oust, and I still possess cognitive and emotional triggers. At times I have to stop thinking such thoughts as, "What if basketball would have worked out?" or "What if I did make it to the NBA?" In fact, it can be emotionally triggering for me to attend basketball games because of the internal emotional reactions that erupt. It is like someone forcefully removing a band aid that covers my wound of disappointment without my consent, and reminding me of a wound that is still in the process of healing. Sometimes when I watch NBA basketball on television, my heart still feels broken and damaged. I find myself battling with you, the menace that's inside. I find myself up against who we once wanted to become. We once wanted to become the player on ESPN playing professionally on television. That's why it hurts when I see current NBA players who we once played with who are now becoming what we did not.

At times, I find myself changing the channel when I come across a familiar face on the television screen. It's sometimes hard to be wholeheartedly happy for them because I am upset at it not being us on television. Sometimes when I come across basketball airing on television it's like redreaming our nightmare all over again. I have at times cried over our disappointment. I have acknowledged our disappointment, and I try to suppress it or ignore it by pretending that I am unbothered when I actually am bothered. I convince myself that I am okay when the truth is, I am not. The truth is, you were never okay so how can I expect us to be okay now. But sometimes we have to be okay with not being okay. It's okay to process, feel, shed tears, and reflect. However, overtime, we are periodically letting go and releasing our menace inside.

Sometimes when our predetermined plans do not work out for our lives, it is neither man nor woman's rejection. In fact, it can be God's divine protection. Sometimes unanswered prayers are simply God protecting us from wrongful desires and plans that do not align with His will for our lives. When our presupposed path leads to a dead-end street, God is simply pushing us to transition down a different path that leads to a destination of fulfillment for our lives. Sometimes the journey truly begins where the road ends. Do not look down and ponder what did not happen. Instead, look up and ask the Lord what is meant to happen in your life. Look up at the Lord and ask Him to transition you to who you were always meant to become. Just because you did not become what you thought you should be does not mean you are not meant to become. In fact, when we do not become what we thought we should be, then it is God's saving grace that allows us the chance to become who He truly created us to be. We must not let who we wanted to become interfere with who we are meant to become.

If we are not careful we can condition ourselves to think and reason like a child. In some cases, we can become oblivious to the danger around us. In times like these, God can act as a cautious parent. As an example, a parent is preparing dinner at a hot stove in the presence of a child. The child becomes curious about the hot stove. As the child reaches for the stove, the parent pulls the child's hand back. The child becomes upset and cries. The child is unaware that the parent saved the child from harm. In the same sense, sometimes we can act just like this child in our everyday lives. Just as the child became curious about the stove and planned to touch it, we can become stirred by what's in front of us and what we plan to reach for in our own lives. We try to reach for what we desire while also being completely unaware that it can burn us. Thus, God can take on the role of an alerting parent in our lives. He will stop us from touching what can ultimately harm us. Don't be a child of God who lives with the thermal burns. Do not reach for plans that God has pulled you back from. Don't turn from the transition that is meant to pull you away from self-harm and direct you to your destiny and purpose.

When we are becoming we must understand that our plans may not be a part of God's plans. A well-known scripture that is often misinterpreted to accommodate our convenience is **Jeremiah 29:11 |NIV| *"For I know the plans I have for you," declares the Lord, "plans to prosper you and not to harm you, plans to give you hope and a future."*** *This scripture both affirms and declares that the Lord already has a blueprint of our becoming. This scripture also indicates that God knows the plans He has for our lives, but gives no clear indication that we will know the plans God has for our lives. And that's okay. Sometimes we will find ourselves in situations not knowing or having a clue where God is taking us. Think of God like a GPS System. Sometimes when we are in route to our intended destination, the GPS will take us on a detour and ultimately recommend a different route. It may not have been where we wanted to end up or the path we intended to take, but sometimes it is right where we are supposed to be.* **Proverbs 16:9-10 |NLT| *"We can make our plans, but the Lord determines our steps."***

God can make it clear that something is not the intended path He has for our lives, but we may try to hold onto it, which can prolong the becoming. It is possible that we can have a destination but no sense of direction. Sometimes we have a sense of compass with no route. At times, we can find ourselves floating through life with no clear direction or destination. This is what I call a fork in the road mentality. A fork in the road is when one path bifurcates and splits into two different directions. This metaphor represents a major choice of deciding which path to choose. Many of us can find ourselves standing in-between two spilt paths. We've been societally conditioned to think one path will be rewarding while the other will be punishing. The ideal is presented that we must choose one of the paths. However, I propose that sometimes neither of these paths may be for us. When it is from God, we won't have to think about which path to choose because there will be one clear path that chooses us. **1 Corinthians 14:33 |NKJV| *"For God is not the author of confusion, but of peace."***

Therefore, I propose that instead of choosing a path, sometimes it is necessary to walk backwards and revisit the footprints that led us to this point. Sometimes it's okay to take some steps backwards so that we can know how to maneuver forward. **May I submit for your consideration, that a step forward in the wrong direction can be a step backwards. However, a step backwards in the right direction is truly a step forward.** *Sometimes a step backwards is a step toward who we are truly meant to become. Sometimes when we step backwards we are actually stepping away from the path that could have been a menace in our lives and closer to the path of our true becoming. Therefore, a step backwards can be a step forward into our becoming.*

Understand, it's okay to take a few steps back by asking yourself, Who am I? What do I want to do and what do I desire? And then ask the Lord, Father, who is it that You want me to become? What am I meant to become? What is it in this world that You have blueprinted for me? What is the path that You want me to take? **Psalm 37:4 |NLT| *"Take delight in the LORD, and he will give you your heart's desires."***

While transitioning into who we are meant to become, we have to remind ourselves that sometimes our taste buds have to mature. When we taste something of ill taste, our initial reaction may be to spit it out. In this case, when God gives us something new to taste and chew on for our lives, some of us respond by spitting it out. However, I am requesting that you digest, not for the sake of the taste, but for the sake of what it can do for your life. Sometimes the healthiest foods can be perceived as unappealing or ill tasting. In the same sense, sometimes God wants to serve us plans that may seem unappealing. However, the plans that God has prepared for us are full of nutrients, supplements, and fibers that will grow and mature us into who He meant for us to become. Sometimes our taste buds have to mature, and perhaps you should again try what God has served you. I am in the transition of maturing my taste buds as well. **John 13:7 |NIV| *"You do not realize now what I am doing, but later you will understand."***

We should be grateful that God did not let us become the very menace that could have harmed us and others. If I had become a professional basketball player in the NBA, I would not be preaching God's word and using my life to help bring souls to the Kingdom of God. Basketball would have eclipsed the very potential and purpose God had for my life. Sometimes what we want to become, can be as detrimental as a Venus flytrap in our lives.

A Venus flytrap is a plant that is able to eat insects using a special technique. To attract flies or other prey, the Venus flytrap secretes nectar on to its open traps. Insects smell the sweet nectar and once they land on the leaves, they trip the trigger hairs on the outside of the traps. This causes the cells in the leaves to expand. In less than a second, the leaves shut and trap the insect inside the plant. In simplest terms, these plants are unexpected death traps for insects. Because the plant appears to have nectar on the outside, insects become oblivious to the lethal trap inside the plant. In the same way, what we want to become can be as deceptive as a Venus flytrap. We may pursue certain things that appear to be beneficial for our lives but can actually be a detrimental trap. Just as an insect is trapped in the leaves of the plant, our purpose and potential is trapped in what we thought would be beneficial for our lives. By the grace of God, the Lord has pulled many of us out of such situations.

I want you to confront the menace inside of you. Forgive yourself for not becoming what you thought you should be. God makes better choices for us than we could make for ourselves. God's plans for our lives are better than any plans we may have so do not be afraid of God's will, even if it is different than your plans. Hold your head high and know that God has a perfect plan for your life's becoming. I currently am in the transition of forgiving myself for not becoming what my younger self wanted to be. Sometimes self-forgiveness is an ongoing process.

Prayer for Self-Forgiveness

Dear Lord, help me release and forgive myself for what I have done and for what has been done to me. Lord, replace this feeling of guilt with peace and serenity, oh God. Help me to know that every step in my becoming is ordained and orchestrated by You, oh God. Father, I ask for Your assistance in letting go of ideals, passions, or habits that no longer complement the frequency of my destiny. Lord, I need Your almighty hand to release my grasp, finger by finger, on the things I cling to so tightly. As I release them to You, Lord, give me all that You have awaiting me. In Jesus name, Amen.

I now challenge you to write a letter to your younger self. As I asked earlier, what is your menace? Your menace can be in the form of a relationship that didn't work out that you may still be longing for. Your menace can be a job, position, or promotion you hoped to achieve but didn't receive. Your menace can be something you aspired to be but you weren't able to become. Again, I ask, what is your menace? Are you still battling with forgiving yourself for not becoming something? How will you use what was discussed in this chapter to help you in your becoming?

_____

_____

_____

_____

WARREN HAWKINS III

. . .

_____

_____

_____

_____

_____

2

The Transition of: Redemption
THE TURN BACK MOMENT

Redemption is the act of regaining or gaining possession of something. It is also the act of redeeming or atoning for a fault or mistake[1].

"Each of us have a turn back moment. It's the moment you either move forward or give everything up. There's one guarantee, if you give up then it will never happen. The choice is yours."—Steve Harvey

When we are becoming, each of us may have a turn back moment in life. It is the moment in life when we decide to keep going after what we desire or choose to settle for what we have. This is the moment when we choose to give up or see how much more we can take. This is the moment when we stand between avoiding the fear of what we think won't happen and the pursuit of everything that can happen. This is the moment we can become discouraged and ask ourselves, "Is this even worth it?" and "Why should I even try?" This is the moment when we question whether to keep moving forward or contemplate turning back. The only guarantee is that if we decide to throw in the towel we are ensuring that whatever we desire will not happen. Each of us transition to a turn back moment at some point in our lives.

Know that it's okay to put the towel down, but it is never okay to throw it away. Sometimes it's okay to sit down, but it's never okay to stay down. It's okay to ask, "Where did I go wrong?" but that doesn't mean we have to believe something went wrong.

If you have ever thought about giving up or have ever given up, I want you to think about why you held on so long in the first place. Because somewhere along the line you believed in yourself. You possessed a knowing so great you believed that what God put in you was meant to come out of you. You once believed you could achieve anything you set your mind to. At one point, anything that was within your reach ended up in your hands and you stretched for anything that seemed out of your reach. Therefore, I ask you, what destroyed your passion? What blurred your vision? What caused you to turn back?

My turn back moment came when I was a junior in college. I was offered the opportunity to preach a sermon to students in our University Chapel. This opportunity was so exciting because I had hoped for it since my freshman year. But when preparing for the service, I became anxious and distraught. Usually when I speak, I am filled with anticipation and excitement. However, approaching this specific event, I felt defeated and unmotivated to preach. I let anxious nerves get the best of me. Every time I shook this overwhelming feeling off, it came right back and gripped me even stronger. I did everything I could to shake this feeling. I watched motivational videos, read my Bible, and even received encouragement from my family and mentors, but no matter what I did to combat this unpleasant feeling, it would not leave.

On the day of the service, I stood on the stage with a defeated mind and a tormented spirit. Because my mind was so defeated, I did not clearly articulate the message God placed in my heart. I stumbled over my words and took deep, loud breaths into the microphone. There were times when I stood silent for long seconds, with my eyes rolled back in my head in a way that

The Transition of Becoming

would suggest I was collecting my thoughts. In fact, the crowd was not oblivious to my frustration. They applauded me and attempted to cheer me on. I heard someone shout, "You got this Warren!" Sadly, their attempts to build me up and give me courage were futile. I was too defeated, and I let nerves and fear get in the way.

After the service, I remember feeling crushed, disappointed, and a bit embarrassed. Not only did I feel like I had let myself down, but that I had let the Lord down. There's a saying that, "time heals" but that's sometimes not the case. Sometimes, time does not heal, all it does is conceal. Sometimes time hides, shelters, and hibernates our pain.

From that day onward, I concealed and hibernated the guilt and failure I felt. In fact, I began to avoid attending chapel services. Each time I entered the chapel auditorium, scenes from what happened on that day replayed in my mind. This was the moment when I had decided to put preaching on standby. This is the very moment when I thought about giving up and turning back from my life's calling and my purpose of preaching the Gospel. I contemplated giving up because I refused to feel that sense of failure that I felt at the chapel. This feeling lay dormant in my consciousness for quite some time. In fact, I endured torment, and emotionally struggled with what happened in the chapel for an entire school year. *Meanwhile, some of us have been battling and holding onto some things our entire lives.*

Winston Churchill once said, "Never give up on something that you cannot go a day without thinking about." So, whatever it is you think about each day is not meant to be just in your imagination. You can achieve the vision God showed you. You can start that business, get that promotion, become an influencer and motivational speaker, pursue your education, and walk in the fullness of who you are meant to become.

Perhaps there is something you may have decided to give up on. Perhaps you experienced a level of disappointment you do not want to relive or even acknowledge. What you hoped for may not have transpired in the way you wanted. You decided to not reach for your star any longer because you did not want to relive the feeling of failure. You did not want to jump again simply because you didn't want to relive how it feels to fall. You did not want to open the door of opportunity because you knew how it feels to reach for a door just to find out it is locked.

I want you to know that anytime you fall you can stand back up. You can spread your wings and try again. I want you to know you can achieve redemption from whatever tried to steal your joy, peace, and happiness. Never confuse pieces of a defeat with a whole defeat. If you run into a wall of discouragement, don't turn back. Figure out a way to climb that wall. Road blocks are not permanent barriers. They are simply blocks that can be knocked down.

When we are becoming, it isn't about avoiding the bruises of life. Sometimes we must collect the scars as a testament of everything we overcame. The stars cannot shine without the void of darkness, and the sun rises and it sets. In order to shine, we may experience dark times and in order to rise sometimes we may fall. If you run into a wall of discouragement, don't turn back, instead figure out a way to climb it. Sometimes we have to fall down in order to understand what it feels like to get back up. We don't have to live with the fear of failure. Failure is an experience and not an outcome. We have the choice of redemption. We have the choice of cleaning up our mess. When we are faced with a turn back moment, we always have the choice to finish what we started.

If we look at the story of Elijah the Prophet in the Bible, we can come to know that he also had a turn back moment. Elijah was a prophet of the nation of Israel. God used Elijah to speak on His behalf and to perform signs and wonders that proved the Lord's existence. However, the miracles God performed through Elijah upset many rulers. A woman by the name of Jezebel, who was a Phoenician princess, threatened to harm Elijah because of the signs and wonders he performed. **1 King 19:2 |NLT| *"Jezebel sent this message to Elijah: "May the gods***

The Transition of Becoming

strike me and even kill me if by this time tomorrow I have not killed you just as you killed them." Out of fear and distress over Jezebel's message, Elijah turned back from the path the Lord had sent him on. **1 Kings 19:3-4 |NLT|** *"Elijah was afraid and fled for his life. He went to Beersheba, a town in Judah, and he left his servant there. Then he went on alone into the wilderness, traveling all day. He sat down under a solitary broom tree and prayed that he might die."* The Lord then spoke to Elijah, instructing him to go back and finish what he started. **1 Kings 19:15 |NLT|** *"Then the Lord told him, "Go back the same way you came."*

Elijah had experienced a turn back moment. Elijah decided to head in the opposite direction from where the Lord intended. Not only did he flee from where he was, but he contemplated giving up. Much Like Elijah, many of us have chosen to flee from our passion and dreams. Many of us have fled because something did not go as planned or expected. In fact, this is what I did after my sermon in the chapel.

As I mentioned earlier, after the incident I felt defeated and a bit shaken up. I put preaching on standby for a few months, and avoided the chapel. I chose not to even attend or be present as a guest or visitor. I did this because I did not want to be reminded of the feeling of failure I had.

The Lord instructed Elijah to return the same way he came. The Lord is instructing us to do the same in our lives. The Lord wants us to go back to the very dream, vision, and goal we fled from so that we can finish what we started. The question is, are you willing to go back? Are you willing to redeem yourself? Are you willing to pick back up where you left off?

Sometimes redemption is like cleaning up broken glass. When glass is dropped it usually breaks into three different sizes. There are the large pieces, medium pieces, and tiny specs. The large and medium pieces are easier to dispose of, whereas the small glass requires us to go back and carefully sweep using a broom. It may be difficult to identify the small pieces, but that does not mean the pieces are not there. In fact, the small pieces of glass are usually *the pieces that cut us simply because we did not see them or think they were still there. In the same sense, many of us have small pieces of glass in our lives that we have not gone back and swept. The small pieces of glass represent a time in our lives when we experienced failure, let down, or some form of disappointment we have not dealt with or healed from. As a result, we find ourselves being cut when we least expect it. Therefore, in each area of our lives we must be sure to sweep up the glass left from anything we experience. In my case, I knew it was time to sweep up the glass I left on the stage in the chapel.*

After some months passed, I resumed my preaching endeavors. Although I continued to grace the stages at other churches, I knew I needed to grace the chapel stage to earn redemption. I knew I had to go back and pick up what was left on that stage and make things right within myself. When the opportunity to preach on the chapel stage presented in my senior year of college. I accepted. I was asked to speak for the last chapel service of the school year. I vowed my approach this time would be completely different. This time I was unshaken, confident, and ready.

The night before the service, I visited the chapel auditorium. The auditorium was pitch black and empty, which was exactly how I wanted it to be. I walked up to the chapel stage and gazed into the auditorium of empty seats. As I stood on the stage, I closed my eyes and imagined myself speaking to the chapel audience. I envisioned how I wanted the service to transpire. I knew I had to be able to see my redemption. I needed to see myself getting back on the stage. *Sometimes we have to close our eyes and see ourselves reaching for what we want. We have to close our eyes and picture ourselves getting back up. Sometimes we have to close our eyes and see our redemption.* I titled my message *Redemption at Its Finest*. I assured the students that they too could bounce back from moments of failure and falling short. I reminded the students that redemption is an option, and they too can move forward.

The Transition of Becoming

What happened in the chapel during my junior year was my turn back moment. I felt relieved and lifted from a burden after speaking for the second time. I had to get back on the stage because what happened in my junior year could have stayed with me for the rest of my life. I knew that in order to fully move forward and heal, I needed to go back the way I came just as the Lord told Elijah. I needed to return to the place where I left a bit of my confidence and passion. I had to get back on the chapel's stage because it took something from me that I could only get back by going back. What was almost a turn back moment became a moment of redemption that kept me moving forward.

You, too, can have a moment of redemption. If you dropped the ball somewhere, go back and pick it up. I need you to be willing to go back and get what that moment of failure or disappointment stole from you. I need you willing to move forward and pick up whatever it was you gave up on. **Understand, that some things in life come not to take us out but to take something out of us.**

An example of this would be the Biblical story of Job. There was once a man named Job who lived in the land of Uz. Job was a righteous and blameless man of God. He was also the wealthiest man, and he lived with his large family and extensive flocks. However, he experienced a turn back moment after some tragic events unfolded in his life. **Job 1:1-3 |NLT| *"There once was a man named Job who lived in the land of Uz. He was blameless—a man of complete integrity. He feared God and stayed away from evil. He had seven sons and three daughters. He owned 7,000 sheep, 3,000 camels, 500 teams of oxen, and 500 female donkeys. He also had many servants. He was, in fact, the richest person in that entire area."* One day Satan noticed that Job was a very blessed man of God. Therefore, Satan went to the Lord asking permission if he could tempt Job. Job 1:9-11 |NLT| *"Satan replied to the Lord, "Yes, but Job has good reason to fear God. You have always put a wall of protection around him and his home and his property.***

You have made him prosper in everything he does. Look how rich he is! But reach out and take away everything he has, and he will surely curse you to your face!"

When we analyze this text, we realize Satan wasn't trying to take Job out, he wanted to take something out of Job. Satan was not trying to take Job's life, he wanted to take Job's love, fear, and adoration for God. In the same way, perhaps you survived something in your life, but maybe the enemy was not after your life. Maybe he was after your praise. Maybe the enemy was not trying to steal your marriage. Maybe he used the challenging times to take the happiness out of your marriage. The enemy was not after the relationship, maybe he tried to use the challenging moments to take your self-love out of you. The enemy was not trying to take you out, perhaps he was trying to take the vision, dream, and passion out of you. The enemy wanted Job to give up on God in the same way the enemy wants you to give up on your dreams and vision. The enemy wanted Job to have a turn back moment on the Lord, in the same way he wants you to turn back on your becoming.

It's Time to Get Up and Walk

In John 5: 3-5, Jesus encounters a paralyzed man lying beside a pool. The disabled man had been lying there for quite a long time. In fact, he had been lying there so long he became comfortable lying on a mat. **John 5:3-5 |NIV| "Here a great number of disabled people used to lie—the blind, the lame, the paralyzed. One who was there had been an invalid for thirty-eight years."** When Jesus saw him lying by the pool he asked him a question. **John 5:6 |NIV| "When Jesus saw him lying there and learned that he had been in this condition for a long time, he asked him, "Do you want to get well?"** Instead of simply replying yes or no, the paralyzed man started to make excuses. **John 5:7 |NIV| "Sir," the invalid replied, "I have no one to help me into the pool when the water is stirred. While I am trying to get in, someone else goes down ahead of me."**

I found the question Jesus asked the paralyzed man to be rather interesting. Jesus may have asked him whether he wanted to be healed because he looked too comfortable in his position. The paralyzed man had a mat to lie on, and seemed too comfortable just lying down. So Jesus asked the man if he even wanted to be healed. Many of us may have the same mindset as the paralyzed man. Some of us have made a mat out of our disappointing moments and have begun to lie down on it. Many of us may lie down because something did not happen as we planned. Instead of living out our dreams, we are lying on it just as the paralyzed man lay on the mat. Just as the Lord asked the paralyzed man, He is also asking us if we want to be healed. The Lord is asking us if we want to dream, have hope, and believe again.

However, just like the paralyzed man, we are responding with excuses. The paralyzed man responded in a way to justify his reason for lying on his mat. And many of us come up with excuses to justify our reason for lying on our mat of disappointment. Instead of saying yes, we come up with every reason why we can't get back up and try again. We come up with any reason why we can't dream. We come up with many reasons why we can no longer believe. We end up lying on our own mat. But no more lying on your mat, it's time to get up. **John 5:8-9 |NIV| Then Jesus said to him, "Get up! Pick up your mat and walk." At once the man was cured; he picked up his mat and walked.**

It's time to get up and walk. Get up from disappointment, get up from failure, and walk back into your dream and the future God has for your life. You may be asking yourself, "What if it doesn't work out?" But what if it does? You may be saying to yourself, "What if it goes wrong?" But what if it goes right? Just get up and walk. The paralyzed man would not have known He was healed and capable of walking if he did not get up. In the same way, how can you be sure your dream won't work out if you are not trying to get up and make it a reality? But just like the paralyzed man, the choice is yours. You can either lie in misery or get up and walk in victory. The Lord had already healed the man, all he had to do was get up and walk in his healing. The victory for the man was predetermined, all he had to do was respond to it. I want you to know that the Lord has already healed you, He has already scheduled your divine breakthrough. He is just waiting on you to pick up your mat and walk.

But you have to be willing to get back up. If I got back up in the chapel, then you can get back up in your business. If I got back up after being broken, then so can you. The option is yours. You just have to be willing to stand back up. There's no reason to look back when you can look forward. There's no reason to ponder on what you think you may have lost, when you have so much to gain. There's no reason to look down on what you think you left behind, when you can look up to what's ahead of you. Get up and try again. This time try again fearless, try again relentless. This time, try believing there are no such things as closed doors, just redirections. Take what was painful and turn it into pain fuel. Use those stones and turn them into milestones. Get back up knowing that defeat is only internal and not external. Sometimes we fear more than we believe. Fear is False Evidence Appearing Real. Imagine if you flipped it. Imagine what you could do. Imagine what you could conquer, reach, and achieve if you used that same energy, not out of fear of what can't happen, but out of belief in what can. *Anytime you may feel like turning back, I want you to say these words to yourself in a mirror.*

Words of Redemption to Say in the Mirror

Today I choose to release everything that has tried to hold me back. I release the past. I release bitterness, hurt, and shame. I release disappointment and missed opportunities. I am enough. I can, and I will achieve what it is that I desire. I will no longer let the misfortune of my past disqualify the fortune of my future. I will release every situation holding me back from my destination. I will look beyond my disappointments and see the divine appointment of blessings, opportunities, and healing God has for my life. I will take what was painful and use it as pain fuel to charge my destiny into existence. I will

The Transition of Becoming

get back up and go after what it is I desire. And if I fall, I promise to get back up again. I will not turn back. Regardless of what I have been through or what has happened in my life, redemption is an option for my life. And as long as my heart beat drums, it is confirmation for me to continue to march toward the rhythm of my becoming.

What was your turn back moment? Have you ever felt like you wanted to give up? Has there been a time when you actually did give up? Has something in your life happened to you that has tried to steal or destroy your praise, dream, or even happiness? Do you have small pieces of glass that you think you need to go back and sweep? Has something happened to you that caused you to feel like it took a piece of you away? When was the moment you were tempted to give up on your plan, dream, or idea? When was the moment you wanted to abandon who you are meant to become? What is it that you need to go back to? How will you pick up your mat and walk? How will you use what was discussed in this chapter to not turn back and step into your redemption?

_____

_____

_____

_____

_____

• • •

WARREN HAWKINS III

3

The Transition of: Embracing
YOUR PROCESS IS CONNECTED TO THE PROMISE

Embrace means to hold someone closely in one's arms, especially as a sign of affection or to accept or support a belief, theory, or change willingly and enthusiastically[1].

When we truly believe we are destined to transition into something great in our lives we may face the challenge of not being able to embrace where we are in the now. Sometimes it's easy to let the promise of who we are meant to become get ahead of who we are becoming in the midst of the process. The expression "cart before the horse" is an idiom or proverb used to suggest that something is being done contrary to its chronological order. The transition to our becoming not only has structure but order. It also has milestones that may become stepping stones. Sometimes God will position us with experiences that allow us to crawl before we walk. Sometimes God will transition us through certain experiences that allow us to grow wings before we can fly out of the nest.

In the same essence, a butterfly is predestined and ordained to fly. That's an inevitable promise to the life and existence of the butterfly. However, before the butterfly spreads it's wings, it must first go through the process of metamorphosis, from being a caterpillar with no wings to being a butterfly who ascends. The promise has already been ordained and appointed on the life of the butterfly, but first it must go through the process. Just like this butterfly, I want you to believe the promise God placed on your life to become has already been predestined and ordained. I want you to believe that just like the butterfly, your wings are inevitable. However, I also want you to learn that in order to manifest the promise of your future, you must first embrace the process of your now.

Every step we take in our becoming has been divinely orchestrated by the Lord Himself. Understand, without first becoming we cannot become. We become not after we have arrived but we are becoming as we arrive. I want you to understand that you have a process that leads to a promise for your life. The process is meant to transition you to the promise for your life. The process and promise are not two, they are one. You cannot get to the promise for your life without the process.

In this chapter of my transition, I have had to learn to embrace where I am now in my becoming. I had to learn to accept my crawling moments, and embrace my moments in the nest. I had to learn to embrace where I am now in the process because it is the only way I will become qualified for the promise.

I published my first book, *Shaped for Greater Works* during my senior year of undergrad college. That following summer, I decided I wanted to schedule myself on a speaking tour. My goal was to travel to different schools, organizations, and churches across the nation to reach people with not only my voice but also with the message of my book. I aspired to speak to auditoriums, churches, and rooms of people. In this way, I was going to see this vision come to pass by any means necessary, even if I had to make it happen. I contacted numerous schools, organizations, and churches in the hopes of being booked as a speaker. In response, I often received the statements, "Who are you again?" ,

"Sorry we don't book locals," or even, "We'll be sure to be in touch with you." Many never got in touch with me. In fact, many times I did not get a response at all. I found myself with a box full of my unpackaged books and unheard sermons and speeches. I became distraught and upset because I had so much passion but no platform. I had sought out opportunities but received what appeared to be opposition. But what I thought was the world's opposition was actually God redirecting my attention.

As I stated, we must not put the cart before the horse. I had to realize that I wasn't letting God lead me, I was trying to lead Him. A cart is not meant to pull the horse. Instead, the horse is meant to lead and pull the cart. In the same sense, we are not meant to pull God. Sometimes we try to put ourselves before the Lord. Sometimes when we are in the midst of transition from one destination to another, the Lord wants us to take a back seat so that He pulls and leads us in the direction He has ordained for us to travel. I found myself trying to pull God to the promise instead of letting God lead me through the process. Anytime we try to pull ourselves to the promise it becomes a heavy burden. When we let God pull us through the process, it becomes a transition that involves faith, trust, patience, and obedience. We are not meant to pull God to our plans, we are meant to let Him guide us to His. I want you to ask yourself, have you ever tried to put the cart before the horse in some part of your life? Have you ever tried to pull God into your plans rather than letting Him guide you into His?

After being turned down to speak numerous times, I felt like I was carrying a burden, but what I was really doing was pulling myself to the promise rather than letting God lead me through the process. We can strain ourselves trying to pick up and carry our process when sometimes we are simply meant to enjoy the ride. I had not consulted God about this book tour. Nor did I search my own heart through prayer to see if it was the will that God had for me in this season of my life. Understand, it is okay for us to dream big. It's even necessary for us to kick down doors of opportunity and reach beyond the extent of our imagination to grab the opportunities we see. It is okay to dream, envision, desire, and believe. However, we have to remind ourselves that sometimes God is meant to pull us before we try to push our way through. Sometimes the first step toward embracing our process is first embracing the process that the Lord has for us. We must embrace where we are now in our process. Sometimes we have to ask the Lord, "Father what is it that you want me to do in this season of my life? Father, is this what you want me to pursue? Lord is this something I am chasing or something you are leading me to? I came to the realization that I was chasing the idea of having a national book tour. It wasn't until I sought the Lord in prayer that I realized I had put the promise before the process and the cart before the horse. We have to be willing to open our mouths and tell God, "Lord, please help lead me in the direction of the path you want me to take. Lord, please help me determine if this is something I want for myself or something that I know you want as Your will for my life." **Judges 18:5-6 |NIV| *They said to him, "Inquire of God, please, that we may know whether our way on which we are going will be prosperous." The priest said to them, "Go in peace; your way in which you are going has the LORD'S approval."***

After consulting God, I realized I had drifted in the wrong direction. I realized the national book tour I had planned was not a part of the process God had for me in this season of my life. I assumed that a national speaking tour was the next step in my process since I saw others taking that path. In a sense, I had compared my process with the process of others. Sometimes we look at other people's promise and compare it to our process. Sometimes we look at other people's footprints and try to follow down their path. Many of us find ourselves comparing our walk with the run of others and our run with the walks of others. We find ourselves never being satisfied with our own pace. We have to understand that their process is their process and that their path is their path.

Jesus understood the power of not comparing thyself. A prophet named John the Baptist was born around the same time as Jesus. As he grew older, John's mission was to prepare people for the coming of Jesus through preaching and performing baptisms. **John 1:23 |NIV| *"John replied in the words of***

Isaiah the prophet, "I am the voice of one calling in the wilderness, Make straight the way for the Lord." John preached and baptized in the name of the Lord. **Luke 3:3 |NLT|** *"Then John went from place to place on both sides of the Jordan River, preaching that people should be baptized to show that they had repented of their sins and turned to God to be forgiven."* During this time, Jesus had not yet begun his public ministry, and there is no proof in the Gospels that Jesus compared himself to John the Baptist. In fact, Jesus did not begin his ministry until he was thirty years old. **Luke 3:23 |NLT|** *"Jesus was about thirty years old when he began his public ministry."*

Often we feel as though God has forsaken us simply because He allowed something to happen to other people and not to us. We begin to make it about our own desires and not the desires the Lord has for our lives. Many times, we put the cart before the horse because we are looking at the carts of others. We can only imagine how much humility it took for Jesus to be the son of God, the messiah, and to not publicly reach his potential until he was thirty years old. And many of us have much potential, gifts, and talents that God is not allowing into the public eye. We must trust God's timing and the process He has set for our lives. We can follow the example of Jesus himself. Jesus understood the significance of embracing His process and moving at the pace the Lord set for him. **John 6:38 |NLT|** *"For I have come down from heaven to do the will of God who sent me, not to do my own will."* *If Jesus could demonstrate the humility to not put the cart before the horse and not move before the Lord, then we can strive to do the same.* **Galatians 6:4-6 |ESV|** *"Don't compare yourself with others. Just look at your own work to see if you have done anything to be proud of. You must each accept the responsibilities that are yours."*

We have to be willing to embrace the path God has mapped out for us. I realized that I was trying to kick my foot in a door, when there was another door next to it already cracked open. In the transition of becoming, sometimes we are not meant to kick down some doors. Sometimes we are simply meant to be still and wait for God to unlock the door He wants us to step into. **Psalm 46:10 |NIV|** *He says, "Be still, and know that I am God."* Being still is exactly what I did. I remained consistent in prayer and no longer tried to solicit speaking engagements without first asking for the Lord's direction. I no longer focused on the doors that would not open but the doors that had begun to open. Instead of me trying to race to opportunities, the hand of God allowed opportunities to meet me in the pace he had set for me in this process. In a matter of days, I received phone calls and emails from local churches in the state of Georgia. They reached out to me with the offer to speak to their congregation. I was soon booked for speaking engagements that occupied me for the remainder of that summer.

I was very proud of the speaking engagements the Lord graced me with. However, they were at local churches with a handful of people in attendance. Regardless of who was or who wasn't in the room, I gave my all because I knew God was in the room. I knew the mission was about the souls at stake. I did not let the emptiness of the rooms discourage me, nor did I falter in my eagerness to preach God's word. In fact, I approached each Sunday efficiently and effectively, well prepared and ready to be an instrument that plays the sweet sound of the Lord's gospel. I approached every speaking engagement with a level of grit and tenacity. At every service, I emptied every bit of what I had in my cup.

Throughout that summer, as a guest speaker for churches, I would often travel to my speaking engagements using public transportation. One late afternoon, I found myself at a Greyhound bus station preparing to travel to a church I would be preaching at the following morning. As I sat inside waiting for my bus, I had with me a duffle bag full of clothes, a box full of my books, and a heart full of the word of God. I began to think about the promise. The promise that I go to bed dreaming about and wake up thinking about. The promising desire I believe the Lord put on my heart. **Psalm 37:4 |NIV|** ***"Take delight in the LORD, and he will give you the desires of your heart."*** The promise that I would one day inspire and reach many in the name of the Lord. The promise that many people's lives will be transformed for the greater good of the Kingdom of God. But as I was sitting inside the bus station, I realized I was about to board a bus most would deem unpleasant. I became a bit distraught. I let my process cause me to doubt the promise. I began to think that maybe I was dreaming too big. That maybe I should start dreaming smaller. That instead of impacting many people for the Kingdom of God, I should only envision impacting a few. Perhaps I was dreaming and aiming too big. Instead of aiming for the stars, I was discouraged to think I should start settling for the clouds. I asked God, "Lord, what happened to the promise?" The Lord then spoke to my heart and said, "You are in the promise, you're just in the PROCESS of doing what was promised." Then the words suddenly came to my mind, "Your process is connected to your promise." I realized that in order to get to the promise we have to go through the process. That our process is connected to the promise, just as the transitions of our becoming are connected to who we will one day become.

I realized that every speaking engagement God allowed me to receive was exactly what I was ready for. When I was speaking to rooms of a few people, this was God taking me through the process of growing my wings before He sent me out of the nest. This was God allowing me the opportunity to learn to crawl before I walked. And in the midst of a baby learning how to walk they may stumble and fall. I realized that I was going through growing pains in my ministry. Although I preached with passion and grit, my sermons still needed to develop before I reached the next level. I'll admit, there were moments after preaching when I realized I needed to go back to the drawing board. Therefore, when we are learning to walk sometimes God will allow us to fall in private and not in public. God will allow us to go through growing pains behind the scenes so the flaws won't show on the big screen. We should never want to arrive too soon. A blessing at the wrong time can be a curse, and promotion at the wrong time can actually be a set up for a demotion. That's why we must let the process take its course. Sometimes we have to remind ourselves to embrace the now of our process. There are no irrelevant or ineffective parts of our process. Each part of our process is meant to equip us with the necessary tools that qualify us for our promise. In the same sense, each stage of the metamorphosis a caterpillar goes through is meant to equip the butterfly with the necessary tools and qualities it needs to become what it was promised to become.

The process is not meant to shake us, it is meant to shape us. The process is not meant to discourage us from our path, it is meant to guide us safely to our promised destination. In order to embrace our process, we have to accept where we are now. Not only accept, but also believe that where God has us is right where He wants us and exactly where we need to be. I understand that sometimes our passion moves before our present and sometimes the future we envision can be what blurs our current vision from seeing what God is trying to do in our lives for the now. I have to continuously remind myself to embrace the now and remember that becoming is a process. Without the process there is no becoming.

1 Peter 5:6 |NLT| "So humble yourselves under the mighty power of God, and at the right time he will lift you up in honor." *There is promise in being in the midst of process. When we are in process we are under the mighty power of God. Each step is ordained and every path taken is a blueprint for us stepping closer to the masterplan He has for our lives. And in the right time, he will lift us up from process to promise.*

Remember, your process is connected to your promise and you are in the process of doing what has been already promised for your life. Your process is your series of transitions which are connected to the promise of who you are meant to become. **My moment of epiphany about my process being connected to the promise that the Lord has for my life comes much later.**

I now challenge you to write about what cart you have put before the horse. What have you tried to pull God into in your life? What in your life have you done that caused you to not consult God first? Was there a time in your life when you tried to rush to the promise rather than endure the process? I also challenge you to write about a time when your process may have led you to question your promise? I now want you to ask yourself, are you aware of your promise? Do you know what your promise is? What is it in this life that you believe God has called you to and for? What do you want to accomplish that you go to bed dreaming about and wake up thinking about?

_____

_____

_____

_____

_____

. . .

WARREN HAWKINS III

Before we enter the next transition I first want to give you a disclaimer. It's okay to believe you are meant to become. Be unapologetic about what it is you want to become. You do not have to dream small, dream big. STOP APOLOGIZING FOR DREAMING BIG! STOP APOLOGIZING FOR THE GREATNESS IN YOU BECAUSE IT IS MEANT TO COME OUT OF YOU!

4

The Transition of: Realization
YOUR PORTION MATTERS

Realization is becoming fully aware of something as a fact. It can also be the fulfillment or achievement of something desired or anticipated [1].

I want you to come to the realization that you do not have to apologize for dreaming big. I want you to come to the realization that you do not have to apologize for your hopes and dreams. I want you to become fully aware that there is a queen in you, a king in you, a beast in you, and an immense level of genius within you. I want you to arrive at the belief that you have been predestined and predetermined to be treasured in the eyes of the Lord. I do believe this for me. However, I cannot believe this for you. I want you to have an undeniable and irresistible level of fulfillment and achievement that confirms that you can and shall win in what you aspire to conquer. The level you see yourself reaching is the level you can climb. You have the abilities to achieve the desires the Lord has placed in your heart. The very script you have written for your life and that you visualize through the screen of your imagination has the potential to become a reality. I want you to come to the realization that you can strive for what it is you want, and that it is okay to believe in what you feel. Whatever it is that you internally see can be meant for you to externally reap.

Many of us have the tendency to look at ourselves as if we are incapable. We tend to look at other people as if they are the lucky ones, and that a certain level of greatness is only attainable to a select group of people. Many of us tend to think, why them? Why not me? If only that was me. I too admit I am both consciously and subconsciously guilty of these thoughts. We can also have the tendency to look at other people and think we don't have the capabilities to achieve greatness. In actuality, we're more than capable. The only difference is, in many cases, they worked for it and believed in it. There are two types of dreamers in this world, those who just believe and those who believe and reach for what they are believing. Sometimes as you're reaching you may fall, you may miss, and you may even stumble, but the one thing you must always do is believe. **Proverbs 23:7 |NIV|** *"As he thinks within himself, so he is."*

What if I was to tell you that God will allow us to live the very life we choose to settle for? That sometimes our external reality is a visual extension of our internal doubts. That sometimes the heights we reach can be a mere representation of how much we are willing to stretch. That how far we've come symbolizes how far we were willing to jump. In essence, there are two types of people in this world: those who take risks and those who don't.

Parable of the Three Servants

Jesus recounts a parable about three servants and their wealthy master. Before leaving his home to travel, the master entrusted his three servants with responsibilities. He gave each of them a share of his wealth. **Matthew 25:15 |NLT|** *"He gave five bags of silver to one, two bags of silver to another, and one bag of silver to the last—dividing it in proportion to their abilities. He then left on his trip."* The servant who received five bags of silver began to invest the money and he earned five more bags of silver. The servant who received two bags of silver went to work and earned two more bags of silver. Both men doubled their wealth through their willingness to be innovative. The third man, who received one bag of silver, hid his money in the ground.

When the master returned home from his trip, he asked his servants to provide an account of the money he entrusted to them. The master was pleased with the two servants who multiplied their wealth and rewarded these two men. **Matthew 25:23 |NLT|** *"Well done, my good and faithful servant. You have been faithful in handling this small amount, so now I will give you many more responsibilities. Let's celebrate together!"* The servant who hid his bag of money pleaded his case to the master. **Matthew 25:25 |NLT|** *"I was afraid I would lose your money, so I hid it in the earth. Look, here is your money back."* The master was not pleased with this servant. He said, **Matthew 25:28-29 |NLT|** *"Take the money from this servant, and give it to the one with the ten bags of silver. To those who use well what they are given, even more will be given, and they will have an abundance. But from those who do nothing, even what little they have will be taken away."* The two men who were faithful with the wealth entrusted to them transitioned into a greater reward, while the servant who was unfaithful had his portion taken away.

Come to the Realization that You Have a Portion

There are many lessons from this parable that can be applied to our lives. I want you to get out of the mindset that greatness is only for certain people. The three servants in this story represent everyday people, and the master in this parable represents God. The bags of silver were given to the three men represent the abilities, gifts, and talents that have been entrusted to us by the Lord.

The Lord gave each of us gifts that are marvelous, magnificent, and valuable. We are each special, unique, and are meant to contribute in this world. Thus, the choice of what we do with our gifts, ideas, and capabilities is entirely ours. We have been given full autonomy to either minimize or maximize what is inherently within us. In fact, the master did not precisely instruct them on what he wanted his servants to do with the bags of silver, he simply entrusted them with it. The master allowed them full dominion and creative control over what was given to them. He did not force or dictate that the servants must multiply their portions.

Again, what if I was to tell you God will allow us to live the very life we choose to settle for? That sometimes our external reality is a visual extension of our internal doubts. That sometimes the very heights we reached can be a mere representation of how much we are willing to stretch. God gives each of us full creative control to either hide our destiny or multiply it into existence. Either we are going to resemble the first two servants or the last.

Come to Realize that Success is Not Exclusive

All three men in this parable were given portions. Many may choose to emphasize how the other two servants were given more than the third servant. However, the emphasis of the lesson was not on the fact that the first two servants were given a larger portion. I believe we can learn a lesson from the second servant. The first servant was given more than the second servant, yet the second servant did not become discouraged simply because the first servant was entrusted with a larger portion. After the first servant multiplied his portion, the second servant realized he too could multiply his portion. Regardless of being given less, he knew he could achieve a level of greatness that he set for himself. He believed in himself enough to increase his portion and achieve a level of success. The second servant did not let having less devalue his portion. In this case, success is not necessarily a product of what we are given, it is a product of what we do with what we our given.

The master punished the third servant not because he still had less than the others. He was punished for devaluing his portion and his unwillingness to prosper what was entrusted to him. The second servant did not let having less stop him from increasing the value of his portion. Therefore, we must not let the thoughts of, "If I only had more I could do more" or "If only I had what they had I'd be better off" stop us from prospering the portion of our gifts and talents.

Many of us can become slighted and discouraged by what others may have compared to what we have. Just like the third servant, you may find yourself in situations where others have been given more than you. Some people come from a privileged environment. There may be people who have more experience, education, and financial stability than you. However, the Lord simply wants you to increase the portion He has entrusted with you. Just because you come from a family who may not have post-secondary education does not mean you can't multiply the portion for your family and be the one who goes to college. Just because you may not have the financial support or stability that you hoped does not mean you cannot start that business. Like the first two servants, make it happen or sit back like the third servant and watch others make it happen. Come to the realization that the best thing you can do for yourself is to do the best with what you have been given.

The word of God proves that if we are faithful with the little we have, we can be rewarded with a bigger portion. God comes to reward not those who hide the innate portion they are given, but those who are willing to work to increase what they have. That is why it is imperative that we tap into our greatness regardless of our situation, circumstance, or past. Come to the realization that regardless of what you have or haven't been given in this life, you have the responsibility to produce, multiply, and advance, increase, or improve the value entrusted to you. Regardless of who you are, where you are from, or what it is that you have been through, you still have value.

Come to the Realization that Fear Will No Longer Hold You Back

The third servant stated, **Matthew 25:25 |NLT| *"I was afraid I would lose your money, so I hid it in the earth."*** Each of these servants were given a bag of silver. The difference is the first two servants had come to a realization while the third did not. The first two men realized they were capable of producing something greater with what they possessed. In fact, they possessed a level of innate belief and confidence in

The Transition of Becoming

themselves that resulted in a rewarding outcome. The two men achieved a level of success and greatness that one did not. Do not let fear of what might happen stop you from believing in what God promised would happen. Do not let fear be the ultimate reason you don't become.

Based on the third servant, I want to ask you: What are you so afraid of? What seed are you hiding in the soil of your doubts? What is holding you back from becoming the best version of yourself? What is stopping you from implementing that creative idea God entrusted with you? What is stopping you from increasing the gifts, creativity, and innovation God has placed within your design? What is stopping you from writing that book? Why haven't you written that play? Why are you still battling the idea of starting that business or launching that brand? Will you continue to hide what's been given to you?

There was a certain point in my life when I also had to come to a realization that my portion mattered, that success was not exclusive, and that fear would not hold me back. When I was a senior in high school someone discovered a portion in me that would be a valuable asset to who I am today. An administrator at school recommended me for participation in a poetry contest. Although the poetry contest was the following day I accepted the opportunity to participate. I only had one afternoon to prepare my own original piece of poetry. My gift and ability for creative writing showed throughout my childhood as I've won school writing contests. I had never written creatively in the form of poetry, but I was confident in my ability. I went home and wrote what was my first ever spoken word poem. At first I found it to be rather challenging, and it took much self-pep talk and concentration. There were moments when I became frustrated and even annoyed. I knew I had a new challenge on my hands that was stretching my abilities. At times, I wanted to stop and just tell the administrator that I no longer wanted to participate. However, I was determined to prove to myself and the Lord that I could do it. I knew this opportunity came with a divine purpose. Although I did not understand the full magnitude of this opportunity, deep down I knew it was something I needed to do.

After a few hours of persistent and focused discipline, I officially finished my first poem. I was proud of myself. In fact, I felt as accomplished as a kid who outgrows his training wheels on a bike. I felt as though I had outgrown a shell and tapped into a new creative version of myself that had value. At the time, I thought I had finished a poem, but really I had opened a portal of new possibilities and gifts that would be used for God's glory. Little did I know, this poetry event would be the grand opening to another side of myself that I never knew I possessed.

On the day of the poetry slam at my school, I was excited and ready. My opposing participants would be other students at my school. There would be a first, second, and third place. My focus was not on placing or on winning but on simply sharing a part of myself that I had newly discovered. I was ready to share what God had placed in my heart. My poem was about the social and cultural challenges of our present-day society.

Most of the high school students were at the event, but I did not feel an ounce of doubt, fear, or nervousness. When it was my turn to deliver my poem, I did just that. I went up to the stage with my poem on three sheets of printed paper. When I finished reading my poem, I received a standing ovation from the audience, and I was chosen the winner of the poetry contest. As stated, I had no intention of winning but on simply sharing my newly discovered and awakened gift. After the event concluded, a well-known poet in the community told me how impressed she was with my poem. She encouraged me to pursue poetry, and invited me to participate in a poetry event she was hosting in the community.

Sometimes God does not require us to take a leap of faith, but to just take a step. And from there, the Lord can take our steps into a plethora of blessings and opportunities. I had never written poetry up until this point in my life. When the opportunity was presented for me to participate, I could have hidden my portion. I could have conjured up excuses and every reason why I should not participate. When preparing the poem became challenging, I could have given up. But I believed my portion of poetry was a gift that had value, and I refused to give up and hide my newly discovered gift. Because I accepted the opportunity and remained persistent, I increased the opportunities for me to grow in my gift. Not only did I win the contest, but another door opened for me to participate in another poetry contest. Sometimes God does not need a leap or a jump, sometimes all He needs is a step.

The following weekend, I participated in my first poetry contest in the community. I immediately realized this was another level of competition and talent. Each of the participants had their poems memorized, and they each possessed a unique style of delivery. The beauty of their word play and their voice inflections made their lines captivating. This form and style of speech was rather new to me. I had never heard speakers deliver words in such a rhythmic way without using a beat or instrumental. In fact, while I watched the other poets perform I, at times, did not understand the metaphors they used. While the audience erupted in excitement and astonishment, I sat there puzzled, still trying to decipher what was so profoundly expressed. As my turn to perform approached, I became distraught. I felt outclassed and even out of my league. Winning my school's poetry contest was one thing, but I now found myself in a room with the best of the best. It was a sudden moment of realization I was unprepared for.

Once again, I stood on the stage grasping my printed sheets of paper. I tried to rely on my memory and not on the paper. Consequently, I stumbled over a few words and at times would lose my place and need to gaze at the poem. I did a poor job in hiding these mistakes. While performing, there were moments when I would make faces and pause awkwardly, which magnified my mistakes. The audience glared and wandered off in different directions. When I concluded my performance, I did not receive the same reaction as my initial performance. Instead, the audience looked rather confused, and hesitated to applaud. My fumbling over words and long pauses caused me to go over the performance time limit. Because this was a competition, I was penalized. Out of eight performers, I placed in the seventh slot. The judges said that the content of my poem was exceptional, but my delivery was amateurish.

I realized my delivery was more like a speech and not a spoken word poem. After being told this and placing second to last I was quite upset with myself. I did not know that spoken word poetry was an art, a craft, and a unique style of its own. Because I had never done competitive spoken word poetry before, I did not know what other way to be, besides who I naturally was. Although I was disappointed, I was also motivated. I was elated that I had discovered a new level to my creative writing and oratorical performance. It was in this humbling moment that I knew I had a lot of work to do.

As I stated, success is not exclusive to a certain group of people. In my first poetry performance in the community, there was a clear difference between myself and the other poets. They had more experience in spoken word poetry. Therefore, I was in a situation that resembled the parable of the servants. The other poets resembled the first servant who had been given the largest portion. I was in a situation where I could have chosen to be like the second servant or even the third servant. After placing second to last, I could have become discouraged and stopped pursuing poetry. However, I knew I could reach the same level as the other poets. I knew I could increase my portion. I knew this level of talent was not exclusive to them, but if I worked hard enough I could also achieve that level of talent. Much like the second servant, although I had less, I did not diminish my opportunity to make more. And that's exactly what I did.

I graduated high school and entered college as a freshman. From there, I became not only a student of academics but of spoken word poetry. I studied spoken word poetry by reading, watching videos of other poets, and by practicing. In order to reach the next level of poetry, I needed to begin with memorizing my poems. As I memorized my poems, I did not speak them as I did when I first started performing. The more I practiced, the more I developed my ability to speak in a rhythmic way. My vocabulary expanded, my writing became more creative, and my ability to use metaphors and punchlines developed. I became more skilled in my voice inflections. I recited poems to the walls of my room, envisioning the walls as the people I would one day perform before.

Over the next few years, I came to the realization that spoken word poetry is essential to who I am and who God has called me to be. As a serious spoken word poet, I have introduced or concluded my sermons using spoken word poetry. When I've spoken on high level platforms or even on television, I have incorporated spoken word poetry into my speech. I became so well versed and skilled that I started to host my own poetry slams in college. I would print flyers, create a list of performers, and partner with food catering organizations to provide food. Many of the poetry events I organized were successful and became popular among students.

One day when I was visiting home during a holiday break from college, I noticed there was an open mic poetry slam taking place in the community. The event was scheduled in the same location where I placed second to last. This time it was not a competition but an open mic showcase. I wanted to attend because I had not performed in my hometown since my second to last place performance. This open mic was traditionally a popular event attended by many of the same poets I initially encountered. This was my moment to show how much I had improved in my craft. This event was personal to me, and I had to make sure I performed.

As the poets performed that afternoon, their talent no longer discouraged me because I also possessed the same talent. I was able to detect and keep up with the word play used by the poets. This time, when something metaphorical was spoken, instead of looking puzzled I responded with the rest of the audience. This time, I knew exactly how to interpret the metaphors.

I recognized many faces from my first community performance, but these many faces did not recognize me. I liked it that way. I wanted a clean slate and to wow the audience with my talent. As I was called up to perform, I did not rely on a stack of papers. I had memorized my poem. Instead of stumbling over words I was able to speak clearly and fluently. While performing, I received many reactions from the audience. They snapped and used verbal gestures that showed they were intrigued. This moment was rewarding because I clearly remembered once being the poet who did not have the audience's attention. But I now became the poet who would say something metaphorical and receive admiration from the audience.

At the conclusion of my performance, I received much applause. As I was on my way back to my seat, I was suddenly interrupted with a warm hug. The person hugging me was the same well-known poet who had watched me perform at my high school. She complimented me on how much I had grown and developed in spoken word poetry. She said she could not believe I was the same poet from a few years ago. Since that day, I have been invited to many open mic events by other poets and community organizers. Churches and organizations have even asked me to perform my poetry for events within the community.

What separated the two faithful servants from the unfaithful servant was the fact that they believed in themselves and the other did not. I was in a similar situation where I could either choose to believe in myself or not. And because I believed in myself and increased my portion, I was able to unlock new opportunities and possibilities for my life.

Every single day you must believe in yourself. Believe in the portion God has entrusted with you. You don't have to be afraid or fearful. You do not have to bury what God gave you in the creativity of your imagination. You don't have to dream small, instead dream big. Why dream small when the reality is that we have a big God? Why only think about a few things when we have a God who can do all things? Why settle when we have a God who wants to do exceedingly, abundantly, and above all that we can ask, think, and possibly imagine. **Ephesians 3:20-21 |NKJV| *"Now to Him who is able to do exceedingly abundantly above all that we ask or think, according to the power that works in us, to Him be glory in the church by Christ Jesus to all generations, forever and ever. Amen."***

I wasn't okay with being known as a beginner in spoken word poetry. I wanted to go above and beyond and reach a new level in my craft. I had the choice to give up on poetry or to increase my portion. Remember, God will allow us to live the very life we choose to settle for. The choice is ours.

Have you ever thought to yourself that success was only obtainable for a certain group of people? Just like the third servant, have you ever been tempted to hide your portion? In fact, what is your portion? Have you ever felt like you hid the talent or gift God entrusted to you? What is something that God has given and entrusted with you that has the potential to multiply? How will you use what was discussed in this chapter to help you realize that your portion matters?

. . .

WARREN HAWKINS III

5

The Transition of: Being Sure vs Being Unsure
THE HAUNTING OF A DREAM

Sure means being confident in what one thinks or knows, and having no doubt that one is right. Unsure is not feeling, showing, or doing with confidence and certainty[1]

"The context of what we see potentially beholds the content of what's yet to come"—Minister Warren Hawkins III

It is okay to be a dreamer! To be a dreamer means our belief in our futures stretches beyond the extent of our current realities and circumstances. I want you to believe that whatever God allowed you to see, He meant for you to reap. God did not sow the seed of your dream in you for it to not sprout out of you. Whatever it is that you see yourself becoming when your eyes are closed is what you can become when your eyes are open. Our dreams are not meant to live in us, instead we are meant to live out our dreams. However, it is always easier said than to believe because being a dreamer can sometimes feel like it is a blessing and a curse.

At times our dreams can feel like they are haunting us. The definition of *haunt simply means: to recur persistently to a place or a thought often revisited. Whenever there's a becoming in our lives sometimes there's no escaping it. When we are meant to become, understand that we are not separate from our dreams. Instead, us and our dreams are one in the same. Our dreams are attached to our very existence. Sometimes when we don't hunt the dream, the dream will ultimately haunt us. In many cases, we can see the mountain top, but become discouraged by the pathway to get there. In the same sense, many of us are sure of the dream God showed us but unsure of how it may happen. We can be sure we are called, chosen, and anointed for greatness but unsure of how it will come to pass. Many of us are sure of who we are meant to become, but sometimes we are unsure as we are becoming.*

Joseph of the Old Testament was known as a dreamer. And much like us, he was in the transition of becoming. Joseph was one of the youngest sons of a man named Jacob. Out of Jacob's many sons, Joseph was the most beloved son. **Genesis 37:3-4 |NLT| *"Jacob loved Joseph more than any of his other children because Joseph had been born to him in his old age. So one day Jacob had a special gift made for Joseph—a beautiful robe. But his brothers hated Joseph because their father loved him more than the rest of them. They couldn't say a kind word to him"*** Not only did Joseph's brothers dislike him because he was their father's favorite, but they also disliked him because of the dreams he began to have. **Genesis 37:5-7 |NLT| *"One-night Joseph had a dream, and when he told his brothers about it, they hated him more than ever. "Listen to this dream," he said. "We were out in the field, tying up bundles of grain. Suddenly my bundle stood up, and your bundles all gathered around and bowed low before mine!"*** Joseph's dream was a revelation of what was soon to come. This dream also implied that God had found favor in him. The meaning of Joseph's dream will be revealed in the following chapter as we continue to unfold the becoming of Joseph.

. . .

The Transition of Becoming

Be Sure that God Purposely Gave You the Dream

I want you to understand that God has given you the dream for a reason. In Biblical times, it was culturally appropriate and typical for the firstborn to have much promise. In many cases, the firstborn son was the son who received a double inheritance, and was the one who would inherit his father's role as head of the family. In the story of Joseph, the reasons for Jacob's oldest son's animosity and resentment toward Joseph are rather obvious. Despite cultural traditions, God still chose to ordain Joseph as the dreamer of the family. The Lord equipped Joseph with dreams that marked him for a divine destiny. I want you to know that God can operate the same way in our lives.

I want you to understand that much like Joseph, God gave you a dream. Joseph was the youngest of many brothers, but the dream was still given to him. Many of us may have moments when we are unsure of the dream simply because we are the youngest or we expect those before us to achieve certain things. However, sometimes the dream may have to start with you. As you read this book, you may be the Joseph of your family. Maybe you are the first person in your family who dreams of generational wealth, graduating from college, or remaining pure until marriage. You may be the dreamer of your family who will be the first one to obtain a doctorate degree, travel the world, or even own a business. Do not be discouraged by the fact that those who came before you did not have the dream. Maybe you are tempted to only become the extent of your surroundings and environment. Maybe you are starting to believe that since no one else before you dreamed beyond their environment, you must follow this same trend. I want you to know that God does not operate on trends. God wants to refine your family line through you. The generational wealth you aspire to build for your offspring can manifest through you. The new trend in your family of graduating college can start with you. God has selected you to be the one to refine and reshape the cycle of your offspring. God may have made your dream dynamic so the reality of your family's dynamics can be changed for the better. God chooses us based on who is capable of restoring order to our family, environment, and communities.

When God gives us the dream, we are not meant to watch others accomplish our dreams. We are destined to fulfill our own dreams. Joseph did not reject his dream simply because he was the youngest. Instead, he embraced his dreams and knew he was destined for greatness. **John 15:16 |ESV| "You did not choose me, but I chose you and appointed you that you should go and bear fruit and that your fruit should abide, so that whatever you ask the Father in my name, he may give it to you."**

Words for a Dreamer

Anytime you feel unworthy or doubtful of the dream, I want you to say these words to yourself: **"I am qualified for the dream. It does not matter what I have been through, where I come from, or what I have experienced. The Lord is going before me and making crooked places straight. My steps will be the footprints that lead those after me to the promise. I am qualified. I will be the example. I will be the exemption that refines the exception for my family and environment. I can and I will be the change I want to see. I am the dreamer."**

Joseph began to dream at the age of seventeen. He did not let himself be limited by what his environment offered him as the youngest son. Joseph did not buy into the expectations society placed on his life. Instead, he believed in himself enough to not let what was usually done discourage him from what was yet to be done. I want you to know that you don't have to fall back just because your circumstances or environment may say so. You can be the exception that refines the expectation. You are never too young nor too old to dream. It is never too early nor too late for you to reach above and beyond what has never been done. The sky is not the limit, instead go beyond. Don't settle for what you can already see, reach above for what you can't see. And just because you can't see it, that does not mean it is not there. Just because it has never been done does not mean you cannot be the first one to do it. In fact, do it even if you are the only one doing it. Dream if you are the only one dreaming. Dream for that business. Dream for generational wealth. Dream to travel the world. Dream for whatever it is that you desire to achieve.

Don't apologize for being the one in your family with a dream. It does not mean you are stuck up, but rather obedient to the dream God placed on your life.

I am the first published author of my family. I am the first male in my immediate family to graduate from college. And as a current graduate student, I will be the first male in my family who will obtain a Master's degree. In addition, I plan to continue my academic endeavors beyond these achievements. Sometimes when we are pursuing a road that has never been traveled, it can be quite discouraging. Although, I've been graced by God with this dream, I also understand that embracing this dream has not been an independent task. I am also grateful I was pushed and propelled into this dream by my mother Katrina and my father Warren II. In my moments of uncertainty, they have had to believe in the dream for me. There were times when my vision became blurred, but they spoke words of vision to help me see clearly. There are times when my hope can float away like a balloon, but they are always there to grab its string. My two older brothers, Keionta and Jaylen, have been a backbone of encouragement for me in moments of uncertainty. They embody the meaning of "I am my brother's keeper." We keep each other encouraged, motivated, and reminded of the goal at hand. Both Keionta and Jaylen are in college and will soon obtain college level degrees. Because we are reaching for the stars, we know it is unacceptable for any of us to settle for the clouds. Not only do my big brothers encourage me, but they inspire me to be great.

As a graduate student, I am enrolled in an advanced and accelerated master's program. This means I will be obtaining my Master's degree over the span of one full school year. There are moments when I feel unsure of the dream. I falter and question if school is worth finishing. But God never promised the dream would be easy. It's one thing to know you were implanted with a dream, but it's another thing to sow hard work to reap the harvest of the dream coming to reality. However, there are two types of dreamers; those *who feel the pressure and give up, and those who feel the pressure and keep going* **Galatians 6:9 |NIV|** ***"Let us not become weary in doing good, for at the proper time we will reap a harvest if we do not give up."***

It's moments like these where we ask, "Why me?" and "Why do I have to be the one?" Well, I want you to flip these questions and start asking yourself, "Why not me?" and "If not me, then who?" I often have to remind myself of these questions. I often have to remind myself of my reason why. My two younger siblings, Amari and Tyler, are constant reminders of why I have to continue to make my dreams not only a reality for me but a standard for them. When I graduate with my Master's degree, they will know they do not have to settle for a Bachelor's degree. They will know they can go beyond what is expected. I want them to know that dreams are obtainable. I want them to believe in what was once deemed out of the ordinary but now has become what's normal for our family. To me, it's about creating a legacy and generating a generational standard. I want them to know that dreams are obtainable. I aspire to make what has never been done become what's expected in our family.

Now I want you to think about your reason why. Think about the people in your family, neighborhood, or environment who are depending on you. Think about those whose hope is connected to your destiny. There's somebody who is counting on you and depending on you. There's someone who may have sacrificed and has pushed and propelled you to where you are today. All they ask is that you pay it forward.

Be Sure to be Careful Who You Tell Your Dreams

But what happens when we have nobody to confide in our dream? What happens when the very people who we thought would dream with us actually are dreaming against us? What happens when the very people we thought would be excited about our dream become intimidated by our potential? This is something Joseph himself experienced. After Joseph told his

The Transition of Becoming

brothers about his dream, they did not respond in a supportive manner. **Genesis 37:8 |NLT|** *"His brothers responded, "So you think you will be our king, do you? Do you actually think you will reign over us?" And they hated him all the more because of his dreams and the way he talked about them."*

Sometimes the courage of our dreams will haunt the insecurities of other people. Not only did Joseph's brothers dislike him because he had dreams, but they also despised him for the way he believed in his dreams. Sometimes people may dislike you not only for your dream, but also because of the level of confidence and belief you possess in your dreams. When you truly believe in your light, sometimes your vibrance can reflect the true colors of others. Because misery loves company, some people will rather you lay in misery than get up and walk in victory. Pay attention to the people in your life who are content with you lying down but disapprove of you getting up. Not everyone will like the fact that you believe in your dream. Sometimes these people will be your closest friends or even family members. Sometimes the same people who you've prayed with and held hands with can be the same ones wishing for your downfall. Sometimes the same people who you think are praying for your future are actually preying on your present.

Your dream holds weight. Not everyone is qualified to carry the weight of our dream. Some people will drop your dream both intentionally and unintentionally. Therefore, it is necessary for us to be careful who we share our dreams with, because some people will be receptive to your dream while others will not. There is no in between. In some cases, it is necessary to keep your dream to yourself. Share your plans with people who you know will nourish your dream rather than people who will suck the life out of your dream. You have the right to be selective with who you choose to carry your dream. **Proverbs 10:19 |NIV|** *"When there are many words, transgression is unavoidable, But he who restrains his lips is wise." In Joseph's case, he told his dream to the wrong people. Beware, sometimes people will project their fears onto you. Sometimes people will tell you that you can't because they never believed they could.*

. . .

Be Sure Even If You Have to Dream Alone

Sometimes we have to dream alone. Joseph had another dream that he shared with his brothers. However, this time he included his father as well. **Genesis 37:9-10 |NLT| *"Soon Joseph had another dream, and again he told his brothers about it. "Listen, I have had another dream," he said. "The sun, moon, and eleven stars bowed low before me!" This time he told the dream to his father as well as to his brothers, but his father scolded him. "What kind of dream is that?" he asked. "Will your mother and I and your brothers actually come and bow to the ground before you?"*** As mentioned, Joseph was beloved by his father and was in fact Jacob's favorite son. The one person we expected to embrace Joseph's dream ended up scolding him for it instead. Jacob scolded Joseph not because he didn't love him nor because he was jealous of him, unlike his brothers. Jacob rebuked Joseph for his dream because he did not understand it.

Many of us have been in a similar situation. We have been scolded by those we expected to support us. Maybe you entrusted someone with the seed of your dream, but instead of planting it in the soil of their encouragement, they buried it in the dirt of their doubt. And they did this not because they didn't believe in you, but because they couldn't recognize the dream you believed in. Sometimes people can only support us as far as they understand us. Sometimes we as dreamers and visionaries are labeled and misunderstood. Sometimes our vision supersedes the sight of other people. That's what happened in Joseph's case with his father. Jacob scolded Joseph because he did not see or understand Joseph's dream. We cannot expect everyone to be able to see the vision God allowed us to see. It may be clear to you and blurry to others. When you are a dreamer expect to be misinterpreted, misunderstood, and even lonely. Sometimes becoming is a lonely road. Sometimes when we are becoming, we are left to believe all alone. Joseph was alone in this moment. The one person he expected to confirm and give him assurance for his dream, scolded it.

When we have no one who is believing in our dream, does that mean we should give up? When people become blind to what God has shown us, do we stop envisioning? When we feel like we are the only ones who believe in our dream, do we stop believing? Of course not. God can make the impossible, possible. At any moment of time, God can put his super on what appears to be natural and can make the supernatural happen for our lives. So sometimes you have to believe in the impossible even when others can only see what is possible. Sometimes you have to believe in the super even when those closest to you only have faith in what is natural. Hold on to a knowing so great that you do not let others shake or falter your belief. God is our gateway but belief is our weapon on the way to the promise God has for our lives. We must use belief as a weapon to knock down the negativity, doubts, and discouragement that may come from other people. Believe in your dream even if you have to believe alone. There may be nights when you will have to wipe your own tears, pep talk yourself, and pat your own back. That's okay, some things we are meant to endure alone.

Be Sure to Let No One Strip You of Your Uniqueness

After Joseph's second dream, his brothers' animosity against him grew stronger. One day when Joseph was approaching his brothers in the fields they planned to seriously harm him. **Genesis 37:18-20 |NLT| *"When Joseph's brothers saw him coming, they recognized him in the distance. As he approached, they made plans to kill him. "Here comes the dreamer!" they said. "Come on, let's kill him and throw him into one of these cisterns. We can tell our father, 'A wild animal has eaten him.' Then we'll see what becomes of his dreams!"*** The text actually says they wanted to harm Joseph because "he is a dreamer." In fact, they didn't even call him by his name. They called him "the dreamer." Many times, people won't necessarily have a problem with us. They have a problem with our dream. They may not be intimidated with who we currently are but with who we set our sights on becoming. As we are becoming, some people will not want to see us become.

Because Joseph was Jacob's favorite son, he gave Joseph a special robe. **Genesis 37:3 |NLT| *"So one day Jacob had a special gift made for Joseph—a beautiful robe."*** This special robe made Joseph unique amongst his brothers, but his brothers decided to strip Joseph of his special robe. **Genesis 37:23-24 |NLT| *"So when Joseph arrived, his brothers ripped off the beautiful robe he was wearing. Then they grabbed him and threw him into the cistern."*** Joseph possessed something that his brothers did not, and they became possessed with stripping him of the very thing that made him unique. Many times, people are going to do whatever they can to strip you of the very thing that makes you unique. They will do whatever they can to get you to believe and think less of yourself. Sometimes when you dream big, they will try to encourage you to dream small. I want you to think to yourself, have you ever had a friend look you in your eyes and tell you that you wouldn't or couldn't? Have you ever had someone try to belittle your idea? Has someone ever tried to plant seeds of doubt and discouragement in you about something you were proud of? This was something that I had to experience for myself.

As a student leader during my undergraduate years in college, I participated in many public speaking forums. One day, I was granted the opportunity, along with two other students, to speak on a national televised platform. Initially, we were asked to prepare individual speeches. However, one of the students suggested we perform a trio speech. The student insisted that it would be beneficial if we all stood at the podium together and took turns reading a collaborated speech. Initially, I was not opposed to the idea, and I accepted the suggestion. We then created an online google word document where we all had visual access to our joint speech. This online google document granted each of us the ability to both view and type out our speeches on the same word document. I pasted my section of the speech onto the online document. A few hours later, the other students told me they did not think my speech was appropriate nor fit the vision they had for our speech. I pleaded my case. I told them they were not in the position to approve or disapprove the content of my speech. They argued against me and then deleted my section of the speech. They then typed in what they wanted me to say in my section of the speech. At that point, I made the decision to no longer participate in the group speech. I decided I would perform my speech individually as originally intended. As a result, they called me selfish and obnoxious. They even gave me smudged and defiled looks throughout the entire event.

I learned many valuable lessons from this experience. I realized they were trying to strip me of the very thing that made me unique. They tried to mold and conform me to what they wanted me to be. And they tried to dim my light. When I did not conform and refused to dim my light, they labeled and name-called me. In the same way, because Joseph kept on dreaming his brothers resented him simply because he had no intention of dimming his light. That's why they labeled Joseph "the dreamer."

Sometimes when people can't control you or understand you, they will try to label you. Sometimes when you refuse to blend in, people will try to make you feel bad for wanting to stand out. This opportunity was a nationally televised speaking platform. Therefore, I had no interest in blending in and conforming to what they wanted me to be. Instead, I had every intention of embracing who God had called me to be. I refused to let them strip me of the very thing that made me unique. This is why we have to remain grounded in self. We have to keep the contract with ourselves and not let anyone strip us of our uniqueness. You are the only one who can break the contract. Don't let anyone encourage you to tear up what you owe to yourself. When we are becoming, there are going to be people who may not want to see us become. They will try to do and say anything to shake us.

Sometimes people will secretly compete with you without you even knowing. Sometimes people will try to dim your light simply because they are not secure with theirs. Many times, people will try to minimize your confidence so that they can feel more secure about the insecurities they battle within them-

selves. This is exactly what happened when Joseph's brothers stripped him of his robe. They were jealous of Joseph and that made them insecure about themselves. In order to help them feel better about themselves, they decided to tear Joseph down. I also learned that moments of conflict can reveal a person's true heart. I learned that it's not always true when people say, "people can say things they don't mean." This is not always the case. Truth be told, they actually meant what they said, they just never intended on actually saying it. **Matthew 15:18-20 |NIV| *"But the things that come out of a person's mouth come from the heart."***

Joseph's brothers were showing the true intentions of their heart. They decided not to kill Joseph. Instead, they decided to sell him into slavery. **Genesis 37:26-28 (NLT)** ***"What will we gain by killing our brother? We'd have to cover up the crime. Instead of hurting him, let's sell him to those Ishmaelite traders. After all, he is our brother—our own flesh and blood!" And his brothers agreed. So when the Ishmaelites, who were Midianite traders, came by, Joseph's brothers pulled him out of the cistern and sold him to them for twenty pieces of silver. And the traders took him to Egypt."***

In the beginning of this story, Joseph was haunted by his dreams. After being sold into slavery, I can imagine Joseph being sure of the promise but unsure of the process that would take him to the promise. I can imagine Joseph being sure of who he was meant to be, but unsure of how he was going to transition to becoming who he was set to be. Joseph was sure he could see the mountain top, but he was unsure of how this path would lead him to the mountain.

The dreams God gives us can represent something that is meant to be birthed into this world. In the early stages of pregnancy, a woman is able to identify that she is pregnant. However, the sex of the child cannot be determined until it develops to a certain stage, nor can they determine what the child will look like. The same works with the dreams God gives us. Some-

times when God gives us a dream, vision, or idea we are able to identify there is indeed a dream within us. However, we are unable to identify how it may look or play out. Joseph had no indication how his dream would play out. Many of us find ourselves in similar situations.

Have you ever had a moment when you felt unsure of the dream? What dream has God given you? Are you the first or only one in your family who has or plans to achieve something nobody else in your bloodline has done? Have you ever felt like you doubted the dream God gave you? Was there ever a time when you needed to be careful who you shared your dream with? Was there ever a time when you felt like you had to dream alone? Have you ever felt like someone or something tried to strip you of your uniqueness?

. . .

WARREN HAWKINS III

_____

_____

_____

6

The Transition of: Redirection
PLATFORM REFORM

Redirection means assigning or directing something to a new or different place or purpose. Reform means making changes in order to improve[1].

"Every time I thought I was being rejected from something good, I was actually being redirected to something better." —Dr. Steve Maraboli
　　What happens when we feel like the dream is being deferred? What do we do when we feel like we are going toward opposition and away from potential opportunity? What do we do when we experience a sudden change of pace and direction in our lives? Sometimes it may feel like we are being set back, but we are really being set up. It may feel like we are being held back, but we are really being pulled back like a sling shot so that we can launch into our futures. When we are in the midst of becoming, we may be redirected on a different path. When we are being redirected, it can feel like God is pulling us farther away from the dream, but in actuality He's bringing us closer to the dream. In this case, it can feel like God is breaking us down when He is ultimately building us up. Redirection is not rejection; it is projec-

tion for our futures. We have to remember that when we are redirected and are experiencing changes in our platforms, it is God reforming something for our destiny.

As a college undergraduate senior, I had much hope and many aspirations as I approached graduation. Because of the success I had achieved during my undergraduate college years, I approached post-graduation with a promising mindset. During my senior year of college, I served as the Student Body President of Clark Atlanta University. This platform exposed me to national speaking platforms that afforded me the opportunity to grace the stage with many public figures. I was also afforded many opportunities to speak on international and national television platforms. I traveled and preached as a guest speaker at many churches. However, God was about to take me through a series of redirections where my platform would be completely reformed.

After graduating college, I enrolled in an advanced standing accelerated curriculum Master's program to obtain my Master's degree in one school year. I started my courses that same summer upon graduating from undergrad college. However, this meant I had to find a real job. I applied to be a paraprofessional, college recruiter, and other jobs. Unfortunately, I did not get hired. The interviewers were not interested in my campus and community involvement. Rather, they wanted to know if I could perform the tasks being asked of me for the job. This was a time of stress because I was in a transition in my life where I was taking on more financial responsibilities. However, I found myself as a college graduate and a Master's student with no job and in a financially vulnerable position. There were bills due in my name that I had to cover. With no direct and consistent form of income at the time, I became financially dependent on the sale of my books and what I earned from preaching engagements. The money I earned from my books and speaking engagements had to be prioritized efficiently. I purchased precooked and canned

The Transition of Becoming

foods. I also purchased a large water jug and occasionally refilled it with faucet water to save money. I found myself in a very testing position. This is not how I envisioned my life after graduation. Prior to graduating college, I had aspirations that were not going as exactly planned. I had high hopes and dreams upon graduation, but I was living a reality check. My life had been redirected, and my platform had been completely reformed. I went from a well-known student body president to an unemployed college graduate trying to find a way.

I was in a similar position to Joseph. He had so much hope and excitement for his future with the way he spoke about his dreams. In contrast, I couldn't help but dream about my future. However, once I experienced being unemployed, I assumed my life had taken a turn for the worse and not the better. As Joseph was sold into slavery, I felt like life had sold me into a reality of disappointment and closed doors. Much like Joseph, my platform was being reformed. Joseph was the dreamer of his family. However, he went from the dreamer of his family to being sold into slavery. His path had been redirected and his platform had been reformed. In my case, I went from a student body president with much promise to an unemployed college graduate.

When we are redirected, it is God taking us through what I call a platform reform. When our platforms change it means God is trying to reform us for the better. This may feel like a curse, but it's really a blessing in disguise. It doesn't mean the dream is deferred, it means there is a divine path God wants us to take in order to reach the destination He has for our lives. When God is redirecting us, He is ultimately taking us through not necessarily where we want to be but where we need to be. This may bring some highs and some lows. This may cause us to experience changes that are discouraging.

In order to grow, God may redirect us through different platforms that reform us as we are becoming. We cannot spread the wings of our destiny while operating in the comfort zone of our nest. Each platform we are given is meant to reform something new within us so we can grow into our full potential. Sometimes when God is redirecting our lives through different experiences, it means we are being prepared and not punished. It means God is trying to shape us and not break us. We are often afraid of change, but sometimes in order to grow we must feel growing pains. Our redirections are lessons, growth, and everything necessary for us to operate in the full capacity of who we are meant to become. **James 1:2-4 |NIV| "Consider it pure joy, my brothers and sisters, whenever you face trials of many kinds, because you know the testing of your faith produces perseverance. Let perseverance finish its work so that you may be mature and complete, not lacking anything."**

After Joseph was sold into slavery, he experienced a serious of redirections. The Ishmaelite traders who purchased Joseph from his brothers sold him to a man named Potiphar, who was an Egyptian officer. Potiphar was captain of the guard for Pharaoh, the King of Egypt. While serving Potiphar as a lowly worker, Joseph's divine favor from God enabled him to find much favor with his master. **Genesis 39:2-3 |NLT| "The Lord was with Joseph, so he succeeded in everything he did as he served in the home of his Egyptian master. Potiphar noticed this and realized that the Lord was with Joseph, giving him success in everything he did."** Potiphar soon made Joseph his personal attendant. He put him in charge of his entire household and everything he owned. **Genesis 38:5 |NLT| "From the day Joseph was put in charge of his master's household and property, the Lord began to bless Potiphar's household for Joseph's sake."** However, Joseph's time with Potiphar soon came to an end. Potiphar's wife falsely accused Joseph of trying to be intimate with her, and Potiphar threw Joseph into prison.

We may look at this trial of Joseph's as a demotion, but it was really a divine set up for a promotion. When we have maximized the potential of our platforms sometimes God has to reform and redirect us so that we can grow. Joseph had excelled and became comfortable in his role in Potiphar's house. If we are only operating in our comfortability we may never rise to our full potential. Joseph had risen to his full potential in Potiphar's house. There was no need for him to overstay. This was not the mountain top for Joseph's life, it was simply a stepping stone. Some platforms in our lives are meant to be temporary. Sometimes where we are in life is a stepping stone to the next transition. The Lord wants us to do exceedingly, abundantly, above what we can ask, think, or imagine in our lives.

Many of us have found ourselves in the same position as Joseph. Maybe you were released from or denied a job or opportunity you wanted. Maybe you were in a season in your life where you excelled and thrived in a certain area or position but it soon came to an end. I want you to know God is not punishing you. He is preparing you. God is not trying to shake your confidence. He is trying to build you with the tools that will equip you with where He wants to take you. We cannot grow and manifest operating on levels of comfortability. In video games, when we master certain levels we are then promoted to the next level. We cannot win the game if we never advance and only continue to operate on a level we've already mastered. We must move onto the next level. In the same sense, once we've mastered a certain level in our becoming, God will redirect us to the next platform in our calling and purpose for our lives. God allowed this to happen in Joseph's life, not to hurt him, but to ultimately help him. Joseph's imprisonment may have seemed like a demotion, but God used it as a device to maneuver Joseph closer to his becoming.

Joseph's favor followed him to prison. **Genesis 39:21-22 |NLT| "And the Lord made Joseph a favorite with the prison warden. Before long, the warden put Joseph in charge of all the other prisoners and over everything that happened in the prison."** Joseph went from being in charge of Potiphar's house to being redirected to prison. He then went from being an actual prisoner to a prison guard overseer when his platform was reformed. Upon graduating college, I expected to do public speaking similar to what I did as the student body president of my university. However, God had different plans for my next transition. Upon graduation and enrolling in a Master's program, God redirected me to a platform that would reform me in a different way.

My Master's level program required me to complete a field practicum experience. This meant I was required to intern at a professional social work agency. I was placed at a crisis shelter that served at-risk youth. The crisis shelter provides holistic services to our population. These services include mental health, substance abuse prevention, wellness, and social empowerment and community service. The experience of interning at a social work agency challenged me and grew me in many ways. Just as Joseph was given tasks and put in charge of Potiphar's house and in the prison, I was put in charge of many tasks and duties that reformed my ministry for the better.

One of the tasks I was given was facilitating group cognitive and behavioral therapy sessions. This meant I would facilitate dialogues to help members cope with and heal from traumatic experiences in their lives. I encountered members of the agency who had experienced heart-breaking trauma that was troubling to hear. I was faced with different personalities, but I was able to see these personalities through an empathetic and sympathetic lens. I realized that sometimes people are the way they are simply because of what they have experienced in life. I was able learn about the psychology of why people may behave the way they do.

This experience not only challenged me emotionally but critically as well. This is when I learned the importance of applying the theories and strategies of clinical professionals. I had to approach these therapeutic sessions with more than just motivational speech but also with research and the correct terminologies. This was not easy. There were many long nights and early mornings when I had to research material to use in preparation for my facilitation groups. This took much disciplined reading and research. This is when my topic of speech began to diverge. Instead of only applying scriptures and motivational quotes to my speech, I learned to apply terminologies and theories that are essential in operating within the social work profession.

I was given a case load of clients. I was in charge of not only assessing their cognitive and behavioral health but also empowering and counseling them through their challenges. This expanded my view on ministry and helped me understand the holistic view of others. Having a case load of clients truly helped me understand the biopsychosocial and spiritual perspective. I was able to access and learn how one's biological, psychological, emotional, and social experiences can impact a person's spiritual well-being. Not only did this experience teach me about individuals, but it also taught me about myself.

This internship taught me organization, structure, responsibility, and teamwork. Both my coworkers and clients depended on me to complete various tasks. Therefore, I had to learn to be punctual and responsible. Overall, there were many times I felt challenged and uncomfortable, but I realized this was much more than an internship; it was a platform reform in my life that was forming my becoming.

This platform reform is forming me for the better. I am learning tools I would have never gained operating on the same platform that I did while I was the student body president of my university. This redirection was not punishment but preparation, and it was not a restraint but a reform. When we find ourselves experiencing platform reform and redirection, God is not trying to tangle us. He is trying to detangle the potential within us that we may have never discovered if we were tied up in comfortable positions. Sometimes when God removes us from a certain path, platform, or position He is not disabling us. Instead He's trying to enable something new within us. Don't be afraid of platform reform as it is meant for you to discover a different form of yourself, just as Joseph began to operate on a new level and discover a new form of himself in prison.

While Joseph was in prison, he utilized his gift of interpreting dreams. This gift gained him favor with the King of Egypt. Pharaoh had experienced two dreams none of his advisors were able to explain. Joseph was able to interpret the dreams. He explained to Pharaoh that his first dream meant seven years of abundance was coming. Joseph told Pharaoh the second dream meant that following those seven years of abundance, the land would experience seven years of famine. Impressed by the wisdom of Joseph, Pharaoh appointed him viceroy, which meant Joseph stood second only to Pharaoh. Pharaoh then tasked him with readying the nation for the years of famine. **Genesis 41:39-40 |NLT| *Then Pharaoh said to Joseph, "Since God has revealed the meaning of the dreams to you, clearly no one else is as intelligent or wise as you are. You will be in charge of my court, and all my people will take orders from you. Only I, sitting on my throne, will have a rank higher than yours."*** When the time of famine arrived, Joseph's God-given wisdom and skills ultimately helped Egypt withstand it. **Genesis 41:47-49 |NLT| *"As predicted, for seven years the land produced bumper crops. During those years, Joseph gathered all the crops grown in Egypt and stored the grain from the surrounding fields in the cities. He piled up huge amounts of grain like sand on the seashore."***

It's safe to interpret that Joseph sharpened his skills at storing grain while being the attendant to Potiphar and the prison warden. Without experiencing those platforms, Joseph would not have been equipped, qualified, nor positioned for his promotion as Pharaoh's viceroy. Each platform God allows us to operate in is not in vain. God may have redirected you to a platform that is meant to reform you. You may be operating in the platform of an intern, assistant, or leader in your church or for an organization. We must learn to embrace every platform God redirects us to. We may think some platforms are unnecessary or irrelevant, but God is using every experience to shape and mold us for who He has called us to be. **Hebrews 13:21 |NLT| *"May he equip you with all you need for doing his will. May he produce in you, through the power of Jesus Christ, every***

good thing that is pleasing to him. All glory to him forever and ever! Amen."

Joseph fulfilled his dreams. During the famine, Joseph's father and brothers were in danger of the famine as well, but because Joseph held such a high rank and favor with Pharaoh, he was granted permission to move his family, including his father and all of his brothers, to a place in Egypt where they escaped the devastations of the famine. The two dreams Joseph had as a teenager had finally come to pass in his adult years. The dreams Joseph had when his brothers' bundles of grain bowed down to his bundle and of the sun, moon, and stars bowing down to him was a prequel to Joseph being the one to save his family from the devastations of the famine.

Every redirection Joseph experienced was not a setback but a divine set up. When Joseph was sold into slavery, he wasn't being deferred from nor denied his dream but redirected toward it. Without the redirections, Joseph would not have achieved his dream. Each platform prepared him for his role next to Pharaoh. Joseph's process was connected to the promise God placed on his life. Sometimes the things we think are working against us are what's actually working for us. The things we think are breaking us down are actually building us up. The things we think are pulling us back are actually working as a sling shot to launch us to where God wants us to be in our future.

Much like Joseph, you are predestined to become what you dreamed. You are meant to become what God showed you. Our dreams are meant to manifest and come to pass. However, we must trust God when he redirects us to different platforms. Do not underestimate or undermine any platform God has called you to. Any platform God gives us can be meant to equip us and qualify us for who we are meant to become. If you are in a season of redirection and platform reform then embrace every bit of it. Be a sponge and soak up every lesson and opportunity of growth so that you can pour purpose and destiny into your future. **Hebrews 10:36 |NIV| *"For you have need of endurance, so that when you have done the will of God, you may receive what was promised."***

There's always a reason for the season and a reform through every platform God gives us. Trusting God's redirection and embracing platform reforms is something I am reminding myself of through my process of becoming. This is not easy, especially if you are a dreamer. Sometimes it's hard to keep your eyes focused on the path when you know you are destined to reach the mountain top. But there's no mountain top without the mountain. **Romans 12:2 |NIV| "Do not conform to the pattern of this world, but be transformed by the renewing of your mind. Then you will be able to test and approve what God's will is--His good, pleasing and perfect will."**

God also makes no mistakes in where He redirects us. Joseph becoming second to Pharaoh and finding favor upon his family was a reminder to Joseph's father and brothers that God had not forgotten about them in the devastating time of the famine. God used Joseph as a reminder for his father and brothers that God still viewed their lives with favor. Sometimes our process is connected to the promise of other people. Sometimes God redirects us so that other people can be reformed for the better.

As an intern at the shelter, I realized God had redirected me so that young souls could be directed back to him. Many of the youth I had the pleasure of serving have experienced trauma and devastating life experiences. I knew this was not only a matter of field placement but a matter of divine placement. I had been placed by the Lord to give hope in an environment that can be full of hopelessness. Therefore, I have taken advantage of every opportunity that presented itself for me to speak hope, life, and light. My internship includes a Bible study with the members of the agency. I tell them that God has not forgotten about them nor forsaken them. I speak uplifting words such as, *"If your heart still beats, that means you beat whatever it is that tried to take you out. You have the victory. The battle is already yours. You just have to believe it."* I would tell them, *"Your story can be used for God's glory. Your story is not a badge of shame, but a testament of how far you've come."* I also told them that, *"Whatever you have been through can be the missing piece for someone else's hope in this life. So never hide the pieces that make up the puzzle of your testimony."* Many of the youth went around quoting some of the encouraging words God spoke through me in those moments of Bible study. Some of them wrote the encouraging words in pen on their hands as a daily reminder of hope and inspiration. Some of the youth started to mention how they prayed and trusted God more in their daily lives. Overall, the seed of Christ was planted in their hearts. And the seeds were beginning to sprout and blossom Christ over their lives.

Not only did I speak out in Bible Study, but I also organized events that empowered them, not just spiritually, but also emotionally and socially. I helped organize open mic events where I encouraged them to write poems and sing songs that helped them therapeutically and creatively express their emotions. I also helped organize a college and career readiness fair. I invited student leaders and organizations from my university to speak and interact with the youth, and remind them that they, too can pursue post-secondary education.

I encountered one youth who reminded me that I was not just there for a practicum experience, but for a divine assignment. This youth was quiet and introverted. Anytime the youth came together in groups, she would just sit in the corner and read a book. She would not utter a word nor attempt to make eye contact with anyone else. Over the course of a few weeks, I began to engage her in individual conversation. She spoke eloquently and was very intelligent. She told me she had read 200 books in her lifetime and that she finished at least one book per week. I encouraged her, and told her I believed in her and that she had what it took to be the author of her very own book. In that moment, her face lit up with a big smile. She told me she had always wanted to write a book, but no one had ever encouraged her to do so. A few weeks later, a note was delivered to me while I was in the office. The note was from her. In the note, she thanked me for believing in her and encouraging her. She had graduated from our services and would not be returning. She was going to proceed with writing a book and telling her story. Her note ended with, *"thank you for believing in me."* I realized I had two roles in this internship. I was meant to be a sponge and soak up all of the information and experiences that I could, but I was also meant to pour out hope and encouragement to the population I was called to serve at the time. As we are becoming, we are meant to help someone else become. Never underestimate the platform that the Lord has given you.

Was there a time in your life when you felt like God redirected your path? Have you ever felt like God took your dream and plans in a different direction than you expected? Is there a time in your life when you felt like God reformed your platform? Have you ever felt like God demoted you from something in your life? If so, how will you use what was discussed in this chapter to trust God's redirection and embrace when God reforms your platform? How will you use what was discussed in this chapter to help you in your life? Did you have an experience similar to mine, where the platform God called you to was meant to help someone else?

_____

_____

_____

_____

_____

The Transition of Becoming

. . .

7

The Transition of: Stride
PACE IS NOT A RACE

A stride is a walk with long, decisive steps in a specified direction, and also a step or stage in progress toward an aim[1].

Becoming is not a race but a stride. We are not racing to become, but we are constantly becoming as we stride at the pace God sets for our lives. It is not a race to the promise but a stride through the process. Stepping ahead or behind the pace God sets is a sign of disobedience. In today's age of social media and instant access to information, it is easy to be influenced to rush to certain things and not stride at the pace God sets for our lives. So many of us are trying to race to the promotion, race to the blessing, or race to certain goals that we set when sometimes God wants us to simply align ourselves with his pace.

Strides are a simple and effective way runners use to pace themselves for a long run. In fact, strides are transitions within themselves. In long distant runs, strides are simply accelerations of speed for about twenty to twenty-five seconds numerous times over the span of a race. Each stride is an attempt to run at about 95 percent maximum effort. After each stride, the runner eases their speed back to a steady pace. Strides are important because they do not fatigue runners by having them run at a maximum speed the entire race. After each stride, the runner reduces their speed to maintain a consistent speed to the finish line without falling behind. Therefore, striding is not necessarily a race but a consistent pace toward an end goal.

Sometimes we are meant to stride when it comes to our relationship with God. There are specific seasons in our lives when the Lord wants us to move at maximum effort toward the desire He placed in our hearts. There are times when God wants us to knock down doors and seek opportunities by applying for the aspired job, creating the website, and handing out resumes and business cards. However, there are also times when God wants us to reduce our speed back to a pace that is consistent with His will by simply moving in a patient and steady pace. There are times when God wants us to slow down and wait on Him to open doors, speak our name into rooms we haven't entered, and prepare stairways that lead to stages. However, when we stride we are never moving backwards or remaining still. We are always moving forward at a persistent pace of hope and faith knowing the finish line is coming. The Bible states in Ecclesiastes that there is a time for everything. I encourage you to know there is a time to accelerate your speed and get what it is you desire, and there is a time to slow down and allow time to take its course.

The problem is, many of us are constantly moving at maximum effort in a rush to promotions, opportunities, and goals. But God may want us to decelerate and move at a consistent pace of faith and patience that aligns with His will. Runners increase their chances of becoming fatigued the longer they run at maximum speed, and they can become so fatigued that it results in a poor performance for the remainder of the race. Because they are fatigued, they delay their arrival at the finish line, Consequently, we can become fatigued from constantly moving at accelerated speeds and this may delay our arrival at the finish line. When we become fatigued from trying to open our own doors and chase down opportunities, we may miss out on the blessing the Lord has for us because we may not have the endurance to make it to the end of the race. We can become frustrated with how long it is taking for God to bring us to the finish line of blessings and opportunities. As a result, many of us quit the race. We quit because we are emotionally and spiritually drained from rushing to the finish line and not striding at a steady pace toward it. If we move ahead of God, in the end we may end up falling short of what God intended for our lives. What we need to know is that the finish line remains the same. God has already predestined you to become. God intends for you to receive what He has for your life. The finish line still stands, so the question becomes, will you?

There was a pressing time in my life when I had to learn to stride and trust the pace of God. When the school year started for my graduate program, I still did not have an actual job. A few churches where I preached in the past were inquiring about hiring me as the youth minister. This was the job I wanted following my undergraduate graduation. However, with each potential inquiry, there was always something that conflicted. Either the church was too far from where I was located for graduate school or the church's requirements conflicted with my graduate course load and internship. In those moments, although it looked as if I was down to nothing, I knew deep down inside that God was up to something. I knew these weren't closed doors but redirections. Although, I wanted to land a youth minister opportunity at one of these churches, I knew this wasn't what God planned for me. I was at a point in my life where I had to stride at the pace God set for my life. I could have tried to run ahead of God and said yes to these opportunities knowing they conflicted with my academic responsibilities. I could have tried to force my foot through the door of these opportunities, but I knew in my heart that I wouldn't have to force myself through the door God had for me. I had to remind myself that the opportunity God had for me would come without confusion and compromise. **1 Corinthians 14:33 |NKJV|** *"For God is not the author of confusion, but of peace."*

Therefore, I had to align myself with the promises of His word and not the pressure of my reality. I continuously quoted **Jeremiah 29:11 |NIV|** *"For I know the plans I have for*

you, plans to prosper you and not harm you, plans to give you hope and a future." In many cases, this scripture can be easy to recite but challenging to endure. I was put in a position where my only option was to endure this scripture. I had to accept the fact that God knew the plans He had for me and that I didn't. And the fact that I didn't know was in fact okay. My one responsibility was to simply trust God. I had to trust and wholeheartedly believe that the plans the Lord had were meant to benefit me. This meant I had to slow down my passion and eagerness and be patient and steadfast. I had to remind myself to not move outside the will of God. What made this situation more stressful and frustrating was that I was at a point in my life where I was striving to be financially stable, but I had to rely on funds from speaking engagements and book sales.

Due to my financial strain, I was tempted to pick up the phone and accept the opportunities presented. I felt pressured to run ahead of God's pace. I was put in the position where I had the choice to either run ahead of God or align myself with His pace. I trained myself to move at a pace of faith. In these moments, I learned to accelerate my faith and trust by striding through moments of discouragement. I had to stride through moments of fear, ambiguity, and uncertainty. I had to stride through moments of feeling like God wasn't hearing my prayers. I did not let the process break me from the promise. I was in a testing moment in my life, but I continued to stride at the pace of God. I knew the finish line was coming in the form of a youth minister job, but my challenge was to not move outside the pace of God. The story of King Saul in the Bible teaches us this.

There was a point in time when the people of Israel wanted a king. God tasked a prophet named Samuel to go out and anoint a King of Israel. God led Samuel to Saul. **1 Samuel 10:1 |NLT| *"Then Samuel took a flask of olive oil and poured it over Saul's head. He kissed Saul and said, "I am doing this because the Lord has appointed you to be the ruler over Israel, his special possession." 1 Samuel***

10:24 "Then Samuel said to all the people, "This is the man the Lord has chosen as your king. No one in all Israel is like him!" Saul is considered the first King of Israel. He was anointed, chosen, and appointed by the Lord. But Saul's downfall came because he did not know how to align himself with the pace of God.

Sometime after Saul became king the nation of Israel found themselves in conflict. Saul and the Israelite army were preparing to go to war against the Philistines. God had promised Saul and the Israelite army that his favor would be with them, and they would be victorious over the Philistine army. **1 Samuel 9:15-16 |NLT| "Now the Lord had told Samuel the previous day. "About this time tomorrow I will send you a man from the land of Benjamin. Anoint him to be the leader of my people, Israel. He will rescue them from the Philistines, for I have looked down on my people in mercy and have heard their cry."** Before going to war, Saul was to wait on the prophet Samuel to arrive so that Samuel could offer a sacrifice to the Lord before they began the battle. While Saul and the Israelite army waited for Samuel to arrive, they became discouraged by the size of the Philistine army. **1 Samuel 13:5 |NLT| "The Philistines mustered a mighty army of 3,000 chariots, 6,000 charioteers, and as many warriors as the grains of sand on the seashore!"** Many of Saul's army ran off and hid out of fear. **1 Samuel 13:6-7 |NLT| The men of Israel saw what a tight spot they were in; and because they were hard pressed by the enemy, they tried to hide in caves, thickets, rocks, holes, and cisterns. Some of them crossed the Jordan River and escaped into the land of Gad and Gilead."**

Sometimes God will put things on hold in our lives to see if we really will trust in Him. God will allow us to wait on something to see if we speed up out of fear that He won't make things happen for us. King Saul and the

Israelite army were in an uncomfortable position that caused their faith and patience in God to be tested. Saul had been promised the victory. However, it seemed as though the longer they waited on Samuel, the more they became concerned about the size of the Philistine army. Many of us find ourselves in the same situation. Sometimes we find ourselves waiting on God and our situation can begin to look worse. The situation began to look worse for Saul simply because his men scattered. Under pressure we have to remind ourselves to remain patient. When we face the pressures of the world, we must lean on the promises of God. However, Saul let the pressures of the world forfeit the promise for his life.

Saul moved outside the pace of God and decided to offer the burnt offering himself. **1 Samuel 13:8-9 |NLT| *"Saul waited there seven days for Samuel, as Samuel had instructed him earlier, but Samuel still didn't come. Saul realized that his troops were rapidly slipping away. So he demanded, "Bring me the burnt offering and the peace offerings!" And Saul sacrificed the burnt offering himself."* 1 Samuel 13:10-11 |NLT| *"Just as Saul was finishing with the burnt offering, Samuel arrived. Saul went out to meet and welcome him, but Samuel said, "What is this you have done?"* 1 Samuel 13:12 |NLT| *Saul replied, "I saw my men scattering from me, and you didn't arrive when you said you would, and the Philistines are at Micmash ready for battle. So I said, 'The Philistines are ready to march against us at Gilgal, and I haven't even asked for the Lord's help!' So I felt compelled to offer the burnt offering myself before you came."***

This was a deliberate act of impatience and disobedience. Saul chose to move outside the pace of God because of the pressures he faced from his army. Likewise, many of us have faced pressures from financial responsibilities, personal or family challenges, and applying for jobs. We may find ourselves financially stressed if we are not approved for a student loan or hired for a job. We must decide if we are going to be paced by the pressures of our problems or the promises of God. We must remain steadfast in the promises of God even while enduring the pressures of our reality. Sometimes when we move outside the pace and will of God it is not bravery or persistence, but an act of disobedience. Sometimes when we move before the pace of God, it can be a sign that we truly do not believe in the Lord's power. It can mean we truly do not trust that the Lord will make a way for us. If you just believe and do not give up, then God will come through for you. **Psalm 27:14 |NIV| "Wait for the LORD; Be strong and let your heart take courage; Yes, wait for the LORD."**

Battle victory had already been promised to Saul. The Lord didn't promise Saul how or when it would happen, but He promised him it would happen. However, Saul felt pressured from the situation, his environment, and those around him to move outside the pace of God. Many of us find ourselves in this same position. We let the pressures of the unexpected cause us to not believe what God already promised would happen.

Paying too much attention to the accomplishments of others also causes us to move outside the will of God. Saul let the size of the Philistine army cause him to doubt what God was going to do for his life and for the Israelites. Likewise, we can let the achievements, content, and even likes of others on social media cause us to move outside the pace of God. Whenever we find ourselves waiting on God, we may look at how others are achieving success, and it may cause us to doubt when the Lord will arrive with a miracle in our lives. As a result, many of us find ourselves taking matters into our own hands just like Saul. We find ourselves moving outside the pace of God to create opportunities for ourselves so we feel like we aren't missing out. That's why many of us are trying to kick down doors that are not meant to be kicked down just yet. The pressures of society are causing us to not wait on God.

Sometimes we make decisions to be validated by people and not approved by God. Don't let social media or the influences of what others are doing cause you to move outside the pace of God just to have something to post rather than truly waiting on something purposeful. We need to realize in this age of social media and instant gratification that it is okay to be still. It is okay to wait on the Lord. It is okay to be still in the reality of our lifeline and *within the content of our timeline. Remember, sometimes we must stride at God's pace and not view life as a race. God is not in a rush, but many times we are. God already promised the victory over your life just as He promised Saul. But the question becomes, will you trust God or will you move outside the Lord's pace and try to force your own way? Will you be like Saul and try to take matters into your own hands?*

Many of us are rushing to shake the next hand, rushing to a big platform or stage, rushing to marriage and relationships. Because of this, we end up forfeiting God's blessings for a life moment of validation. And that's exactly what Saul did. **1 Samuel 13:13-14 |NLT| *"How foolish!" Samuel exclaimed. "You have not kept the command the Lord your God gave you. Had you kept it, the Lord would have established your kingdom over Israel forever. But now your kingdom must end, for the Lord has sought out a man after his own heart. The Lord has already appointed him to be the leader of his people, because you have not kept the Lord's command."*** *If Saul had moved at God's pace and not his own, he would have reached the full potential God had for his life. If Saul had remained consistent with God's pace and not tried to run ahead, he would not have fallen behind. Because of this decision, God selected another man to take Saul's place as king.*

We can look at this story as an example of a false start in a race. In the beginning of a race, each runner is lined up behind the starting point. As the runners take their positions, they eagerly await the signal for the start of the race. However, if an anxious runner moves just before the official sounds the signal, that runner is penalized or even disqualified and they may never reach the finish line. This is exactly what happened to Saul and this is also what happens to us in our everyday lives. Many of us are penalizing ourselves simply because we are anxiously moving before God directs us to. We can become so anxious in wanting to reach the finish line that we run before God signals us to go. We can become disqualified or penalized from what God had planned for us. Remember, pace is not a race. You are not in competition with anyone for your destiny. God has you on your own individual track. And as you line up to start the race, your only competitors are anxiousness and impa-

tience. In Saul's case, his competition or threat was not the Philistine army. His anxiousness and impatience turned out to be his downfall.

In this moment of my life, much like Saul, I was tempted to move outside the pace of God. I wanted so desperately to land a youth minister job. I felt God had put the desire in my heart, and I knew it was going to come to pass. However, I remained disciplined and grounded in the pace God set for me in this season of my life.

Do you have a Saul mentality in a certain area in your life? Was there a time in your life when you moved outside the pace of God? Were you ever in a situation similar to me, where you wanted something but you had to wait on God? Have you ever felt the pressures of wanting to move before God? Have you ever felt pressured by society to chase opportunities so that you could feel validated by people and not approved by God? How will you use the story of King Saul to not move outside the pace of God?

_____

_____

_____

_____

_____

. . .

The Transition of Becoming

8

The Transition of: Patient Expectation
THE WAITING ROOM

Patient (patience) is the ability to endure difficult circumstances such as perseverance in the face of delay, while expectation is a strong belief that something will happen or be the case in the future[1].

At some point in our becoming, we will find ourselves in a waiting room. A waiting room is a specified area where people sit while waiting for things, such as a doctor's appointment, a bus, or even a flight. For example, for a doctor's appointment, after the patient checks in at the front desk, they are seated in a waiting room. Here the patient is asked to wait until the designated professional calls for them to proceed to their appointment. The waiting period is not only critical for the patient but also for the professional. While the patient is seated in the waiting room, the professional is organizing and working in another room to prepare for the scheduled appointment. The patient may not see anything progressive happening, but just because the patient does not see it does not mean the professional isn't already preparing for the scheduled appointment. What's interesting is that the patient not only waits, but waits with an expectation. The patient does not question nor doubt their scheduled appointment. Therefore, to be a patient usually requires a level of expectation. This not only takes expectation but faith and trust. The patient puts full faith and trust in knowing and believing this waiting room is only temporary. The patient expects and believes their name will soon be called and their scheduled appointment will happen.

There are times in our becoming when we must act as God's patient and sometimes He will transition us in a waiting room. In this sense, we are the patient who has been designated to sit in God's waiting room and wait with an expectation that He will call our name. The Lord is the professional who is preparing for our scheduled blessing, promotion, and moment of favor. If we can have the expectation that a human will call us out of the waiting room, then why can't we have the same expectation that our all-knowing and all-powerful God can as well? Understand, it's okay to expect. In fact, the Lord wants us to approach Him in full expectation, trusting and believing what He said will come to pass. However, the Lord also wants us to be grounded in patience. In this moment of my life, I was in a waiting room. As I still did not land a youth minister job, I simply knew that I needed to wait with patient expectation.

After being offered various youth minister jobs that conflicted with my academic responsibilities, I decided to humbly decline the offers. However, I did not stop believing in the Lord. I knew my wanting to take on the responsibility of a youth minister was not a mistake. I remained grounded in this season of waiting. I'll admit, this wasn't easy. There were moments when I became frustrated and upset with the Lord. I had thoughts of giving up on my youth minister aspirations and applying to different types of jobs. I felt the Lord had forgotten and forsaken me.

One day I called my mother and father. I told them I was beginning to lose hope in this period of waiting. My parents encouraged me to not throw in the towel. They reminded me that God had not forgotten about me, and if I truly believed God wanted me to be a youth minister in this season of my life then it was meant to happen. They suggested I utilize job search websites. At first, I was against the idea. I thought that if I couldn't land a minister job with churches through personal relationships then I could not expect to land one as an unknown candidate applying with a resume.

In that moment, the Lord spoke to my spirit. I felt the Lord tell me, "Do not limit me to what's expected." I realized I was putting a limit on God and a Biblical reference came to mind. **1 Kings 17:2-4 |NLT| *"Then a message from the Lord came to Elijah. It said, "Leave this place. Go east and hide in the Kerith Valley. It is east of the Jordan River. You will drink water from the brook. I have ordered some ravens to feed you there."* 1 Kings 17:2-6 |NLT| *"So Elijah did what the Lord had told him to do. He went to the Kerith Valley. It was east of the Jordan River. He stayed there. The ravens brought him bread and meat in the morning. They also brought him bread and meat in the evening. He drank water from the brook."*** *Ultimately, the Lord had blessed Elijah in an unusual and unexpected way. The Lord had allowed ravens to feed Elijah.*

There are two lessons we can take away from this story. The first is that the Lord uses the unexpected to bring us the blessings we expect. The Lord is not limited to what we expect. Instead He sometimes chooses to show His glory through what is unexpected. Elijah found himself without food and water. We'd expect that the last place Elijah needed to be was in a dry and deserted wilderness. Not only that, the Lord also told Elijah that he had ordered ravens to feed him in this wilderness. Typically, humans feed birds, birds do not feed humans. However, the Lord is not limited to what is expected. Instead, the Lord shows up in unexpected ways. **Ephesians 3:20 |NIV| *"God can do anything, you know – far more than you could ever imagine or guess or request in your wildest dreams!"***

Another lesson we can learn from this situation is that Elijah was in a waiting room himself. The Lord gave Elijah an expectation. The Lord told

The Transition of Becoming

him he would be fed, but the Lord did not clarify the exact time Elijah would be fed. When Elijah arrived in the valley of Kerith, the ravens didn't come to feed him until the following morning. Elijah had to wait on what was expected. He had to wait on what was already promised. Elijah had to wait in a waiting room knowing his scheduled appointment to be fed would happen. Elijah remained patient in his expectation. And because he remained patient in what was expected, he was able to receive what was promised. I want you to never falter in your expectations for God fulfilling what He has promised to you. The Lord has not forgotten nor forsaken what He has promised for your life. Your blessing is closer than you think. Your breakthrough is around the corner. Your joy shall cometh in the morning. Much like Elijah, you may be hungry for what God has promised, but soon the Lord will bring you a full course meal of blessings and promotion.

We have to remember to remain patient while expecting God to deliver what was promised. Sometimes we try to put God on an expiration date. Just as one orders something in the mail, there is an expectation that it will be delivered. In addition, an expected arrival date is usually given. We cannot approach God as if the Lord is a mail deliverer. In some instances, the blessings and promises the Lord has for us may not come with a delivery date but simply an expectation that it will be delivered. We have to trust that what we ordered through our prayers, thoughts, and the words of our journals will be delivered. The expected date we want to receive something may not be the date the Lord has divinely scheduled for us to receive it. Yes, we should have expectations that what God promised will indeed happen, but sometimes it is necessary for us to release our expectation for how it will happen and our expectation of when it will happen. Just believe and know it is going to happen. God will make it happen at the right time, in due time, and on His time. **Isaiah 60:22 | NLT |** *"At the right time, I, the LORD, will make it happen."*

Elijah's story encouraged me, and I took the advice of my parents and began to look for youth minister positions on job search websites. After scrolling unenthusiastically, I came across a nearby church that was seeking a youth minister. I met every requirement listed under the job description. The church was seeking someone who was licensed in the ministry, had obtained a bachelor's degree, and was passionate about preaching the word of God. In that moment, I felt assured that this job was a portal to the new beginning I prayed for. I knew this would be the youth minister job the Lord had for me. I sent my resume to the listed site and then waited for a response.

I found myself in a position of waiting once again. While waiting on God in a certain area of our life, we can become so anxious that we become distracted and neglect other areas of our lives. To help take my focus off waiting for the church to respond, I remained grounded in my other responsibilities and obligations. I kept reading my Bible and remained consistent in my individual Bible study. I continued to give my full effort in my graduate level courses. I became so busy with my other responsibilities that I was not consumed with waiting for a response from the church.

One day when I was in class I realized I had an email from the job website I used to apply to the church. The email was sent as an alert to remind me that I had an interview scheduled the following day. The church I applied to had emailed me a few days prior informing me that I had been approved as an official candidate for the youth minister position. The email also informed me that I would have a phone interview with some of the staff of the church. I quietly said to myself, "Thank you Lord." I knew it was by the grace of God that I did not miss the notification from the church.

In that moment, I realized that when we wait in patient expectation, God will never let us miss the opportunities He has for us. The Lord will put us exactly where we need to be to receive what it is that He has for our lives. What caused me to see that the church had reached out to me was a follow up email from the job search website notifying me that the church I applied to had scheduled an interview for me. I realized this was divine intervention. This was more than a follow up from the job website, this was a follow up from the Lord Himself. We must realize that when God has our name on a bless-

ing, it can't miss us and it won't miss us. At first, I was waiting on the opportunity. Then God flipped the tables to the opportunity waiting on me.

When we remain patient in the waiting room, it will not go in vain. Whatever is meant for us, He won't let it pass us by. Sometimes God doesn't operate on open or closed doors. Rather, He operates in the sense of revolving doors. A revolving door typically consists of three or four doors that hang on a central shaft and rotate around a vertical axis. The revolving door cannot be closed or shut. The opportunity to walk through the door remains constantly revolving in a circle due to its structure. When an opportunity is solely for us, the Lord won't just open a door, He'll set before us a revolving door. All we have to do is walk through it. **Revelation 3:8 |NIV| *"I know your deeds. See, I have placed before you an open door that no one can shut. I know that you have little strength, yet you have kept my word and have not denied my name."***

The day of my phone interview with the church arrived. In preparation for the interview, I prayed, meditated, and got dressed in a nice suit. Although, the interviewer staff wouldn't be able to physically see me, I was in the mindset of making a great impression. I believe in the philosophy of, *"If you look good, you feel good. If you feel good, you play good."* And I had every intention of performing well for this interview. This was much more than an interview to me. This was an opportunity to step closer to my life's calling and destiny. Therefore, I did not approach it lightly. I not only wanted to prove to myself that I could do this, but also to the Lord that I was not taking for granted the opportunity He placed before me. Therefore, every part of this interview was serious to me.

After interviewing with a few of the church representatives over the phone, once again I found myself sitting in a waiting room. If I was selected to move forward, I would receive correspondence from the church. Although I believed I had performed well, there was no guarantee that the church would correspond with me. Once again, I had to remain grounded and in patient expectation. I had to remain patient while expecting that the Lord would bless me with this opportunity. A few weeks later I received correspondence again. The church notified me that this time they wanted to conduct an in-person interview. After the in-person interview, I had to wait for the church to contact me once again. After several weeks, I received notification that I would progress to the final stage of the selection process. I was to preach a test trial sermon to the youth of the church to determine if I would be selected for the position.

Once again, I approached this opportunity seriously. I prepared my sermon weeks in advance. Since I would be preaching to youth close in age to my two younger siblings, Amari and Tyler, I decided to get their feedback. I consulted them about some of the challenges youth their age experience. I wanted to approach this final stage with my best effort and no regrets. When the day arrived, I preached my sermon to the youth, and once again I went through a waiting period. Several weeks passed and I had not received any correspondence from the church. In fact, more weeks passed than the other waiting periods for the previous interviews. At times, this caused me to become anxious and a bit rattled, but every time my mind started to think about a negative outcome, I focused on the positive. Many times, I found myself on the ground praying to the Lord. I would say, "Father, what you have for me, will not miss me. I did everything to the best of my ability. Everything else from here on is in Your hands." And sometimes that's all we can do. We have to remind ourselves to hand it over to God. And once I fully released it to God, the Lord released it back to me. One day, when I was working on a class assignment, I received an email from the church informing me that I had officially been hired as the youth minster of the church. **Philippians 4:6-7 |NKJV|** *"Be anxious for nothing, but in everything by prayer and supplication, with thanksgiving, let your requests be made known to God; and the peace of God, which*

The Transition of Becoming

surpasses all understanding, will guard your hearts and minds through Christ Jesus."

I dropped my knees on the ground and my face to the floor. The Lord had finally called my name out of the waiting room. Expectation that I believed in God had finally come to pass and being patient had finally paid off. It's one thing to have expectations, but it's another thing to have patient expectation. Not only did I have to fully expect God would deliver, but I also had to wait in patience knowing that He would. Patient expectation is expectation that does not waiver nor falter. It is expectation that remains consistent in faith and stands firm on the promises of God. Expectation in believing that what God promised will indeed happen. I felt rewarded, grateful, and assured. I felt that the Lord rewarded my patience and diligence. I felt grateful because this was exactly what I had prayed and asked the Lord for. Not only did I finally have a job, but I landed a job connected to my destiny. I knew this was where the Lord had ordained me to be. Unlike the other church opportunities, this position came without me having to compromise my academic commitments. I felt as though God had exceeded my expectations. Understand that God sometimes has us in a waiting room because what He has for us exceeds what we were expecting.

In the New Testament, Lazarus, who had two sisters named Mary and Martha, became very sick. The two sisters sent a message to Jesus that their brother was sick and they asked Jesus to heal Lazarus. Jesus did not come immediately, and Lazarus passed away. **John 11:4-6 |NLT| *"But when Jesus heard about it he said, "Lazarus's sickness will not end in death. No, it happened for the glory of God so that the Son of God will receive glory from this." So although Jesus loved Martha, Mary, and Lazarus, he stayed where he was for the next two days."***

Mary and Martha found themselves in a waiting room. Unfortunately, while waiting on Jesus to arrive, Lazarus passed away. This looked quite bad for the sisters as this wasn't the outcome they expected. It seemed that waiting on the Lord had resulted in the death of Lazarus. Many of us can find ourselves in this same situation. There are moments when we think waiting on God has caused something in our lives to pass away. There are moments when we can think the dream, promotion, or goal has passed. However, I want you to know that whatever you think has passed away in your life, your dream, vision, or idea is not dead because God is about to wake it up. **John 11:11 |NLT| *Then he said, "Our friend Lazarus has fallen asleep, but now I will go and wake him up."***

When Jesus arrived, Lazarus had been dead for four days. Both of Lazarus' sisters felt that if Jesus had arrived sooner he would not have died. **John 11:21 |NLT| *"Lord," Martha said to Jesus, "if you had been here, my brother would not have died."* John 11:32 |NLT| *"When Mary reached the place where Jesus was and saw him, she fell at his feet and said, "Lord, if you had been here, my brother would not have died."*** However, this was in the Lord's will. If Jesus had healed Lazarus when they first requested, it would have been a common miracle. At this time in the life of Jesus, He was performing tons of miracles especially in healing diseases and sicknesses. But the Lord had every intention of raising Lazarus from the dead and performing a miracle that was unexpected. **John 11:43-44 |NLT| *"Jesus called in a loud voice, "Lazarus, come out!" The dead man came out, his hands and feet wrapped with strips of linen, and a cloth around his face."***

When the Lord raised Lazarus from the dead, it was a miracle where nobody could deny the power of God. In that moment, Lazarus, Martha, and Mary were all blessed beyond what they expected. They did not expect Jesus to raise Lazarus from the dead. The Lord had exceeded their expectations and the Lord wants to exceed your expectations as well. Although they had to wait a little longer, they received a greater miracle. Maybe the Lord is taking a little longer than you expected because He wants to give you better than what you asked for. Anytime God has us in a waiting room, we can expect bigger and better than what we prayed and asked for. Martha and Mary originally expected a healing, but what they ended up receiving was a revival. Remain in patient expectation when you are in the transition of a waiting room. The

Lord will bring you what you expected, and He may exceed your expectations if you believe and remain patient.

Prayer for Patience

Lord, grant me the patience as I await Your answers to my call. Teach me to be calm in the midst of a storm. Lord calm the waves of my thoughts and allow me to be still in the breezes of Your peaceful presence, oh God. Just as the waves wash the shore, Lord I ask that You wash away all anxiety, doubt, worry, and fear that lie in the shore of my subconsciousness. Lord, help remind me that my joy shall cometh in the morning. Teach me, oh God, to trust Your sense of timing and not my own. Give me a listening ear that waits for the voice of Your direction. Whisper gently like the wind into my soul, and blow breezes of peace and serenity over my life. Lord, I know You are for me, on my side, and will never leave nor forsake me. Amen.

Was there a time in your life when you found yourself in a waiting room? Have you ever had to wait on something from God that you knew would arrive? Were you hopeful? Did you trust? How will you use what was discussed in this chapter to help you in times of waiting on God?

_____

_____

_____

_____

. . .

WARREN HAWKINS III

9

The Transition of: Heart Alignment
QUALIFIES DIVINE ASSIGNMENT

Alignment is the arrangement in a straight line, or in correct or appropriate relative positions, or a position of agreement or alliance. Qualified means fitted for a given purpose[1].

Heart alignment qualifies us for the divine assignment God has for our lives. When our hearts are properly aligned with God's will and path for our lives, then it qualifies us to be used by God in a mighty way. If our hearts are not aligned with the Lord, then we can disqualify ourselves from becoming who and what God has for our lives. Think of heart alignment with the Lord as a horse race. In a horse race, each contestant is given their own lane for the race. Each contestant is required to stay within the alignment of the lane given to them. If a contestant drifts outside their lane, it may result in a penalty for the race. This can apply to our walks with the Lord. Whenever our hearts drift outside the lane of God's will and plan for our lives, it can penalize us from what He has for us at the finish line.

In order to truly become who God wants us to be, we have to be all in with God's plan and will for our lives. The only way to be wholeheartedly for the Lord is for Him to have our hearts. **Matthew 6:21 |NIV|** *"For where your treasure is, there your heart will be also."* Treasures are anything that is highly valued and considered precious. In order to be qualified for the divine assignment the Lord has planned for our lives; we cannot value anything more precious than the Lord Himself. In fact, pleasing God and aligning ourselves with the will and plan He has for our lives should be our treasure, even when it is hard and gets challenging. And if we value the Lord as what is most precious, valuable, and sacred in our lives, it is only then that God truly has our hearts. If our treasures are in anything else, then that is exactly where our hearts are. The problem is, many of us hold other things as treasures before the Lord. This can lead to our hearts not being aligned with the Lord.

It is possible for your job, a relationship, business, or even a goal to become a treasure in your life. Anytime we value anything more than God, it means He doesn't have our hearts. The reason many of us drift outside of God's will and plan is simply because our hearts are in other treasures. Instead of looking forward in the race at what the Lord has for us, we begin to drift out of the Lord's intended lane for our lives. Just as in a horse race, we'll find ourselves drifting away from what the Lord had for us at the finish line simply because we didn't remain aligned with Him.

Proverbs 4:23 |NIV| *"Above all else, guard your heart, for everything you do flows from it."* When our hearts are aligned with the Lord, then certain qualities will be revealed through our actions. As stated, my goal was to land a youth minister job at a church. Although this was the goal I so eagerly wanted, I did not move outside God's pace and I remained patient in expectation. In the previous chapters, I stated how I had decided to humbly decline a few youth minister job offers. Although, I had a goal in mind, I had alignment with God's will in my heart. There were times when my heart could have drifted out of the lane of patience the Lord had me in. I could have responded with the King Saul mindset. I could have moved outside of God's pace and anxiously accepted a youth minister job that God did not intend for me to have. I also mentioned that the church where I was eventually hired involved a waiting room process. My heart could have become contaminated with impatience and lack of faith.

I could have turned back to the jobs I had declined or even given up while waiting on the church to correspond with me. Because I did not move outside the pace of God and remained patient in expectation, this was an indication that God had my heart. Although other treasuring opportunities presented themselves, I did not give in because I valued aligning myself with the Lord's will as my treasure. And because the Lord was the treasure of my heart and not achieving the goal itself, this meant my heart was aligned and qualified me for the divine assignment of becoming a youth minister. **Psalm 20:4 |NIV|** *"May he give you the desire of your heart and make all your plans succeed."*

As discussed in the previous chapters, because King Saul of Israel had displeased God, the Lord would soon anoint a new king to take his place. **1 Samuel 13:13-14 |NLT| *"How foolish!" Samuel exclaimed. "You have not kept the command the Lord your God gave you. Had you kept it, the Lord would have established your kingdom over Israel forever. But now your kingdom must end, for the Lord has sought out a man after his own heart. The Lord has already appointed him to be the leader of his people, because you have not kept the Lord's command."*** This new king, and soon to be successor of Saul, was a young man named David. David was chosen to be king because of his heart.

After Saul displeased the Lord, the prophet Samuel set out to anoint the new soon-to-be King of Israel. The Lord told Samuel to visit the house of a man named Jesse and that the new king was one of his sons. **1 Samuel 16:1 |NLT| *"Now the Lord said to Samuel, "You have mourned long enough for Saul. I have rejected him as king of Israel, so fill your flask with olive oil and go to Bethlehem. Find a man named Jesse who lives there, for I have selected one of his sons to be my king."*** The prophet Samuel did as the Lord commanded. When he arrived at Jesse's house to anoint the son who would be the king, he discovered seven sons of Jesse. Samuel approached each son in an attempt to anoint him as the new king, but with each attempt, the Lord informed Samuel that none of these sons were the ones God had chosen to be king. **1 Samuel 16: 6-7 |NLT| *"When they arrived, Samuel took one look at Eliab and thought, "Surely this is the Lord's anointed!"But the Lord said to Samuel, "Don't judge by his appearance or height, for I have rejected him. The Lord doesn't see things the way you see them. People judge by outward appearance, but the Lord looks at the heart." 1 Samuel 16:8-10 |NLT| "Then Jesse told his son Abinadab to step forward and walk in front of Samuel. But Samuel said, "This is not the one the Lord has chosen." Next Jesse summoned Shimea, but Samuel said, "Neither is this the one the Lord has chosen." In the same way all seven of Jesse's sons were presented to Samuel. But Samuel said to Jesse, "The Lord has not chosen any of these."***

The Lord rejected each of Jesse's sons, but Samuel knew the Lord was true to His word and there would be a king anointed out of Jesse's sons. Samuel asked Jesse, "Are these all the sons you have?" Jesse replied, "There is still the youngest, but he's out in the fields watching the sheep and goats." Samuel demanded that Jesse send for him. Once David arrived, the Lord told Samuel that David was the chosen one amongst his brothers. Samuel anointed David as King of Israel in front of all of his brothers. **1 Samuel 16:13 |NLT| *"So as David stood there among his brothers, Samuel took the flask of olive oil he had brought and anointed David with the oil."***

As the youngest brother, David was the least likely candidate and he was not initially considered a contender to be king. We can conclude that David qualified for this divine assignment because of what the Lord told Samuel after rejecting the first brother, Eliab. **1 Samuel 16:6-7 |NLT|** *"When they arrived, Samuel took one look at Eliab and thought, "Surely this is the Lord's anointed!"But the*

Lord said to Samuel, "Don't judge by his appearance or height, for I have rejected him. The Lord doesn't see things the way you see them. People judge by outward appearance, but the Lord looks at the heart."

Samuel made the mistake of assuming Eliab was qualified to be king from looking at his outward appearance. Samuel was ready to anoint Eliab based on his height and not his heart. However, the Lord does not promote us based on what is on the outside, but what is on the inside. Many of us think what we portray or our outward appearance overshadows what is hidden inwardly. Maybe the Lord has not allowed you to receive what you are asking for simply because He sees something in your heart that may be displeasing to Him. The Lord may not be concerned with how well you speak or sing or how talented and intelligent you are. The Lord may not be concerned with how many followers you have on social media or how many professional connections you may have. The Lord is more concerned with what people can't or may not see. The Lord is more concerned with how you treat people, your actions behind closed doors, and what you say about people when they are not around. Each of these actions are true reflections of your heart. We may find our lives stagnant and still because our hearts are not right with the Lord. Understand, we cannot hide any thoughts, malicious intent, or agendas from the Lord. **Jeremiah 17:10 |NLT|** *"But I, the LORD, search all hearts and examine secret motives. I give all people their due rewards, according to what their actions deserve."*

In today's age, it is easy to have the mindset of David's brothers. Many of us think we become qualified solely on outward appearance. This causes us to think that just because we have entrepreneur in our bio on social media or have a creative website or even an impressive resume that it will qualify us for God-given opportunities. That is the world's way of promotion, but not the Lord's way. It is not about what you have in your social media bio, it is about what you have in your heart that qualifies you in the Lord's eyes. **Psalm 75:6-7 |NLT|** *"For exaltation comes neither from the east. Nor from the west nor from the south. But God is the Judge: He puts down one, and exalts* *another."* If we are not careful, bitterness, entitlement, and arrogance can flow from our heart. The Lord is able to see under the foundation of our makeup and is able to see what is loose in our lives behind nice ties. **Proverbs 4:23 |NIV| *"Above all else, guard your heart, for everything you do flows from it."***

People do not qualify you, God does. Jesse originally did not think of David as the contender for king. If it was not for Samuel asking Jesse if he had more sons, his father would never have thought of David. His father undermined David by not even referring to him by his name, instead calling him "the youngest." Outwardly, David's brothers appeared to be more qualified than David. In the same sense, other people may appear to be more qualified than us in certain areas of our lives. Someone else may have a higher position, a longer resume, speak more languages, or even have more credentials. But remember, God does not see how humans see. When your heart is aligned with God, nobody can disqualify you from what God has qualified you for.

What made this so unique is that David was a shepherd boy, but he was also anointed king. As the newly anointed King of Israel, this meant David would no longer tend to a pasture but ascend to a palace. This meant David would go from the shepherd of sheep to being the shepherd of a nation. As a shepherd, David was responsible for watching over the sheep on a farm. Unlike his brothers, David was willing to be in the fields and that qualified him to take the throne. David's brothers wanted the palace but wanted no part of the pasture. David's brothers wanted to shepherd a nation, but they did not want to first shepherd sheep. David's heart was in the process which qualified him for the promise. David wasn't just in it for taking a seat at the table but also setting up the table.

Ask yourself, is your heart in it just for the seat at the table, or is your heart humble enough to set up the table? Are you willing to endure what it takes in the process so that you can become qualified for the promise? God is looking to promote and elevate not those who feel entitled to the promise, but those who are willing to endure the process. God is looking to qualify not those who want to become, but those who are willing to transition as they are becoming.

. . .

Transitions for Heart Alignment with the Lord

1: Honesty

Proverbs 27:19 |NIV| *"As water reflects the face, so one's life reflects the heart."*

In order to align your heart with the will of God, you must first be absolutely honest with yourself. Examine your thoughts, actions, and emotions. What are your intentions and motives? Have you defiled others in your speech? Do you genuinely want to achieve certain things because you believe the Lord placed the desire in your heart, or are you chasing your own desires? Do you want success for you, or do you want it for the validation and approval of others? Have you ever felt entitled to something? Have you ever felt like something was owed to you? Do whatever you have to do to be absolutely honest with yourself. Ask these questions out loud, to yourself in a mirror, or even answer these questions in your journal.

2: Ask

Psalm 51:10 |NIV| *"Create in me a pure heart, O God, and renew a steadfast spirit within me."*

Ask the Lord to search your heart and create a pure heart within you. Ask the Lord to cleanse your heart of anything that may be displeasing to him. Ask the Lord to wash away anything in your heart that is not of Him. Also ask the Lord to replace your desires with the desires He has for your life.

3: Submit

Job 22:21 |NIV| *"Submit to God and be at peace with him"*

Submit to the will and plans the Lord has for your life. Submission is a process which calls for us to deny ourselves the power of privilege that we may want. Submission is an ongoing discipline. To submit is "to obey, put under, be subject to, submit oneself unto, put in subjection under or be under obedience or obedient to." Just as a military troop submits to the orders of the head sergeant, we must submit to the plans of the Lord. In this case, we are choosing not to always try to make things happen for ourselves, not to always

try to control and dictate people or situations, but instead to humble ourselves under the Lord's authority, wisdom, and power.
Sometimes submitting requires silence and isolation. Sometimes it is necessary that we quiet all of the noise around us and spend alone time with the Lord. In order to hear God, sometimes we need to put ourselves in a situation where nothing can interfere with us hearing His voice. Spend this alone time praying and speaking to the Lord. Also spend this time reading the Lord's word. Submitting also requires patience. Sometimes we won't have all of the answers after praying and that's okay. Sometimes things won't change nor get better overnight. This is when we remain steadfast in prayer and faith in the Lord. Lastly, submission requires release. We must be willing to release our plans, desires, and anything that is blocking our hearts. We must be satisfied with giving our all to him. In the military, the troops do not try to give the head sergeant direct orders. In the same sense, we should not try to order and direct God. There can only be one chief, and that is the Lord himself.

4: Commit

Proverbs 16:3 |NIV| *"Commit your work to the LORD, and your plans will be established"*

Remain committed to this same process. Heart alignment is an ongoing transition that we may revisit often in our lives. We have to stay committed to the process of first being honest with ourselves in everything we do, what we are praying for, and what is happening in our lives. We must commit to asking the Lord to help create in us a pure heart that is aligned with His will for our lives. Lastly, we must always remember to remain submitted to the Lord. Even if we experience success and opportunity, never forget that the Lord brought these blessings and opportunities. Sometimes we may be in a position in life that may call for us to resubmit. If you feel as though your heart is drifting away from the Lord, resubmit to His will and plan by being honest, asking, submitting to his will, and remaining committed.

Do you believe that your heart is aligned with the Lord? Are you willing to align your heart with God's process for your life? Are you willing to align with the plans of the Lord? Be honest and write about a time in your life *when you felt as though your heart might not have been aligned with the Lord. Have you ever had the mindset of David's brothers? Have you ever felt entitled to a certain blessing or opportunity? How will you use what was discussed in this chapter to make sure your heart is aligned with the Lord?*

_____

_____

_____

_____

_____

_____

_____

_____

_____

10

The Transition of: Starting from the Bottom
PASTURE BEFORE PALACE

If you are reading this right now, I believe you can reach above and beyond for what you dream of. I believe the very star you see yourself reaching is the very star you can grab and hold. Whatever level you see yourself reaching can be the level you achieve for your life. As stated, you don't have to dream small, dream big because we serve an even bigger God. I believe you can be successful in the business you want to own. I believe you can achieve that promotion. I believe your vision can come to pass. Although I've stated that it is okay to dream big, I also must remind you that sometimes we must start small. In today's society, starting small isn't necessarily deemed laudable or praiseworthy. In today's generation, it is easy to want the promise but no part of the process that comes with it. But sometimes we have to be willing to serve in a pasture before we ascend to the palace.

In the last chapter, I recounted how David was a shepherd boy who served in a pasture. Then he was anointed King of Israel and ascended to a palace. David started at what can be considered the bottom. "Started from the bottom" means to be in a position of coming from humble beginnings and working your way up to where you've always aspired to be. It means working from a lower state of being to a higher state of becoming. Being a shepherd boy was not praiseworthy, laudable, and was taken for granted. In fact,

David seemed to be on the bottom of the hierarchy. David's willingness to pasture first qualified him for the palace because he started from the bottom as a shepherd boy tending to a pasture. In the same sense, many of us have a pasture that we are tending to. Your pasture being your business plan, idea, ministry, or even YouTube channel.

Your pasture is the very thing God has you attending to. Your pasture is the very book you aspire to write; it is the very idea you know can change the world. Your pasture may be the church group God has called you to minister. Whatever goal, idea, dream, or vision you have, that is your pasture. You may feel as though you are starting from the bottom with your pasture. However, I want to change your perspective on what it means to "start from the bottom." We have to start somewhere, and it is better to start somewhere than not start at all. It is better to write your book even if it may not sell as much as you hoped than to not write it at all. It is better to keep hosting that Bible study even if only four people attend than to not host it at all. It is better to start your speaking career even if you have to start off speaking to those around you than to not speak at all. It is better to upload inspirational videos even if your content only reaches a few people than to not upload it at all. I want to remind you that just because your dream or vision may start off small does not mean God does not have bigger plans for it. Just because you have only sold a few books, only been an intern or volunteer at a company or business, just because you may have only a few subscribers to your YouTube channel, or only a few customers in your business, does not disqualify your pasture from its potential to become a palace. But in order to ascend to the palace, we have to be willing to tend to the pasture. In order to ascend to the top, sometimes we have to be willing to start from the bottom. **Zechariah 4:10 |NLT| "Do not despise these small beginnings, for the Lord rejoices to see the work begin."**

There's something about the pasture that we must not take for granted. There's something about starting at the bottom or even small that is meant to teach us. What if starting small with your dream was God's plan for your life because He wants you to learn something that will be useful later? What if God wanted your dream to start off at a pasture level because there's something about the pasture that you'll be able to utilize in the palace? Well, I *want you to know this is also true for our lives. Although you have plans for owning the company, the reason God may have you interning is because there's something He wants you to learn that will equip and qualify you. Although you want your business to reach the world, God has only allowed it to reach those in your circle because there's something you need to learn about being small that can help you become big. Sometimes starting at the bottom teaches us how to stay at the top.*

This is not only true Biblically in the life of David but also culturally. Tyler Perry is a world-renowned producer, director, actor, screenwriter, playwright, and author. One day, I came across a video of Tyler Perry delivering a very impactful and motivational speech during the 2019 BET Awards. While accepting his award of *Ultimate Icon Honor*, he said something that really stood out to me: "So while you're fighting for a seat at the table, I'll be down in Atlanta building my own." Tyler Perry was referring to the studio film lot he built, which is one of the largest in America and is known as Tyler Perry Studios.

I truly appreciated his words because in that moment his words became a reminder and a dose of motivation for me. His words truly resonated with me and reminded me that dreams do come true, and when we are willing to work hard enough we can achieve greatness. After being inspired by those words, I thought to myself, Tyler Perry can't be too much different than any of us. He, too, once started somewhere. He too must have started at the bottom. Much like us, he must have a pasture that led him to the palace of his own studio film lot. And in that moment I thought to myself that if he can go from pasture to palace, then so can I.

I began to research Tyler Perry's story. I came to learn that before Tyler Perry became world-renown, he started off local. He began his career during the early 1990s writing and directing stage plays. This was his pasture. Although Tyler Perry had a pasture, he had every intention of stepping into a palace. Even in the beginning of his career, Tyler Perry wanted to open his own studio lot. He had dreams and visions of being big. He had no intention of ever being small. Much like us, he faced discouragement while tending to his pasture. In an interview, he talked about the challenges he faced when he organized local plays for the community. He stated, "I thought 1,200 people would show up that weekend but only 30 people showed up." Moments like these were the times he became challenged and discouraged. Even with dedication and much hard work, Tyler Perry did not see the results he wanted right away. In the same interview, he stated, "From 1992, 1993, and 1994, I was doing one show a year. I kept on doing the play. Every year it would fail, until 1998, the seventh year of me trying. I was about to give up and walk away."

Regardless of the lack of attendance at his plays, Tyler Perry knew his pasture had the potential to become a palace. He kept tending to his pasture. Instead of quitting and giving up on his pasture, Tyler Perry used his pasture as an opportunity to learn, grow, and evolve. He started asking his audience members for feedback and what inspired them most about his plays. According to Perry, "My life shifted after that. My intention became, how do I serve other people? How do I lift other people?" From there, Tyler Perry's audiences grew to thousands of people. He went from having empty seats to having sold out venues for his plays. He starred in and produced films and directed stage plays until he became one of the most credited entertainers. He now owns his own studio film lot, the dream he envisioned for himself since the beginning of his career.

Therefore, we can learn from Tyler Perry's story. He saw his pasture as preparation and not punishment. He saw the lack of attendance not as a closed door but an opportunity to open a door of lessons and growth. Asking his audience for feedback propelled him forward. By enduring his pasture, he learned how to be effective for his palace. Sometimes we have to fail at the bottom in order to be sufficient at the top. Sometimes we have to fail in our pasture so that we can be sufficient in our palace. Don't look at your pasture as inefficient or irrelevant. The pasture is meant to prepare you for the palace.

Sometimes we have to develop in private before we are broadcasted in public. Think of your pasture as a dress rehearsal. Without a dress rehearsal when it's time to take the stage you will still be trying to figure out what to wear. By the time the curtains open and the spotlight hits you on the stage, you want to already be dressed.

I've not only spoken to you as the reader but also myself as the writer. In my case, I have minister aspirations for my future. However, right now I am learning to tend to the pasture because there is something about this pasture that can help me evolve into who God predestined me to be.

I am tending to my pasture as the youth minister of a church. As a youth minister, I have the responsibility of preaching to the middle and high school students every Sunday. As a youth minister of what can be considered my own flock, this opportunity is allowing me to learn some vital information and experiences that will be needed for my future aspirations. I am learning the importance and value of preaching sermons and teaching lessons every Sunday that enhance the spiritual growth of the youth in the church. I also teach Bible lessons that enhance their Biblical knowledge and understanding. My pasture is full of growth, lessons, and opportunity.

My responsibilities are, at times, very challenging. I have to develop a sermon theme for each new month. After picking the topic for the month, I craft lesson plans for every Sunday that fit the selected topic of the month. This has been a challenging task within itself, but taught me the importance of organization as I craft weekly comprehensive and structured sermons for my audience to understand.

Given that I was preaching to middle and high school students, I came to understand the importance of knowing my audience. In order to keep the young people engaged, I had to be creative and my lessons had to be out of the ordinary. I used props and different creative demonstrations not only to make my sermons fun and engaging, but also because using visuals helped the students understand the lessons. I knew that in order to reach them I needed to do things that were of them. In fact, I approached this opportunity modeling the philosophy of the Biblical evangelist Paul. Apostle Paul is considered one of the greatest evangelists of all time. In the Bible, Paul travelled and preached the Gospel to many nations. His ministry became multiethnic, multicultural, and multigenerational. He knew that since he was approaching people of different ages, cultures, and social classes, he needed to reach them with the Gospel by becoming what they were. **1 Corinthians 9:22 |NIV|** *"When I am with those who are weak, I share their weakness, for I want to bring the weak to Christ. Yes, I try to find common ground with everyone, doing everything I can to save some."* Paul understood the importance of becoming what the audience needed so they could receive Christ. In the same sense, I understood that young people needed creativity, illustrations, and even fun in order to increase their interest in receiving Christ.

Not only am I a minister inside the church, I also find myself being a minister outside the church. There are times when I support some of the youth of my congregation by attending their sporting events. This teaches me the importance of building relationships with members and families of the congregation. After services, I speak with the parents of the youth and discuss the spiritual growth of their children. Not only am I able to build relationships, but I also earn experience in event planning.

As a leader of the church, I also sit on the leadership advisory board. During these meetings, I have the opportunity to learn how churches receive donations and sponsorship. I've also learned how churches organize and plan events for the congregation and community. While participating in these meetings, I learned the importance of working with a team. There are times when the other ministers and I work together and plan events for the church. Each of these experiences become lessons of growth and wisdom that I believe will be beneficial both now and in the future.

Sometimes we can be so focused on the palace that we don't take time to appreciate the pasture. Therefore, stop trying to race to the palace and be willing to walk through the pasture. Appreciate and embrace your pasture. The pasture is meant to teach us what the palace cannot. Instead of focusing on how you can elevate to the next level, ask yourself what you can take away from the level you are currently at. Instead of thinking about how to elevate, focus on enduring the stage in your life you are at now. Maybe the internship is meant to teach you how to one day run the company. Maybe serving as a volunteer will equip you with knowledge and skills necessary for your future. Maybe shadowing under mentors is equipping you with the knowledge and tools necessary for you to one day step into the full potential God expects. Start asking yourself, "What can I learn from this experience?" , "Lord what is it you want me to take away?" and "Father, what is my pasture meant to teach me?" **Luke 16:10-11 |NIV| "Whoever can be trusted with very little can also be trusted with much, and whoever is dishonest with very little will also be dishonest with much."**

While tending to our pastures, it sometimes can be challenging to remain faithful to our vision or dream when we may not get support. Because we live in an instant gratification generation through social media, it can be easy to seek validation from others. We must not focus on who does or does not believe in our pasture. We must not focus on views, likes, reposts, or even validation. Do not get discouraged if your pasture is not getting the attention you want. Don't let the fact that some people may not believe in you or how others may overlook you shake the foundation of your belief in self. God does not promote us based on whether other people believe in us. God does not promote us based on the number of social media likes or reposts we receive. In fact, the Lord promotes us based on how faithful we are to the pasture. Remember, all of that ties into outward appearance, but the Lord looks at the heart. The Lord promotes us based on our willingness to serve in the pasture. The Lord honors us based on our willingness to host the Bible study even when only two attendees are in the room. God honors us based on our willingness to start the

YouTube channel with only a few subscribers. The Lord promotes us based on our willingness to start off small. The Lord promotes us based on our willingness to start at what society deems the bottom.

David did not let others' disbelief in his pasture stop him from tending to it. As stated in the previous chapter, when Samuel asked Jesse, "Are these all the sons you have?", Jesse undervalued and overlooked his son David. He said, "Well, there's the youngest but he's out in the fields with the sheep." Jesse was David's father, but he still undermined and overlooked the potential of his pasture. In the same sense, some of our closest friends and family may not see the potential of our place in our pasture. They may not see the potential of our business in the business plan. Others may not see the potential of our ministry in the pasture of Bible study. Don't be discouraged if people do not see the potential palace in your current pasture. People may not see the promise of who you are meant to become, as you are becoming.

David's family only saw a boy tending to the pasture, but God saw a man who would soon ascend to a palace. They saw a boy who was a shepherd to sheep, but God saw a man who would shepherd a nation as the king. In Tyler Perry's case, many people only saw the empty seats, but he ended up becoming a man who filled arenas. Many people saw a man who only wrote plays, but he ended up becoming world-renown and owning his own studio film lot. Therefore, we must tend to the pasture no matter the odds. People may only see your business as a hustle, but God may see it as a soon-to-be prominent company or business. People may only see you as a workaholic, but God sees you as someone who will reach and inspire the world. People may only see a business plan, but God may see it as a thriving business. Others may only see a YouTube channel or motivational post, but God may see a purposeful ministry. Never underestimate your pasture. Tend to your pasture because it has the potential to become a palace. Tend to your pasture even if you have to do it alone. David was out in the pasture alone. Even if you have to do it alone, do it! If you have to start the business by yourself, then by all means do so. If you have to execute your plan by yourself, then do what needs to be done! Regardless of who supports you, God has already approved you for your palace, you just have to stay faithful to the pasture. It does not matter who does not believe in you, *the Lord has already anointed you for the promise. You just have to remain obedient in the process.*

Lastly, never underestimate your process. Understand that your pasture has the potential to be the hope and blessing for other people. David becoming king would be the hope of all of Israel. David would go on to become one of the greatest kings of Israel. Many people depended on David. God also did many great things through him. When Tyler Perry opened his own studio, he believed God was using his studio to help others. When he opened his own studio, Tyler gave many young actors, actresses, screenwriters, and playwriters the opportunity to tend to their pasture and follow their dreams. Remember, sometimes our process is connected to the promise of other people. Sometimes we must become so that we can help others become. You cannot give up because if you do then so many other people may lose. Someone is counting on you to tend to your pasture. Your destiny can be the missing puzzle piece that solves someone else's purpose and hope in life. If you do not finish the race, people who come behind you won't know where or how to start. Someone is depending on you. Someone is connected to you. Someone out there is depending on your pasture because it has the potential to become their palace.

What is your pasture that has the potential to become a palace? Have you tended to your pasture? Have you written the book? Have you started the YouTube Channel? Have you started the business? What is your dream, your vision, or the idea you have been keeping dormant in your mind? What is the very thing that God has placed in your heart to do? Is it a business? A ministry? A restaurant? How will you tend to your pasture? How will you learn to appreciate your pasture? After reading this chapter, how will you use what you learned to help you embrace the process of your pasture? How have you learned to appreciate the beauty of starting from the bottom?

. . .

The Transition of Becoming

11

The Transition of: Pressing
BEING WINE PRESSED

Pressing means to apply pressure to something to flatten, shape, or smooth it, typically by ironing. Pressing may also be a device for applying pressure to something in order to flatten or shape it or to extract juice or oil[1].

A winepress is a device used to crush grapes and extract juice from within them. Wine makers use the machine for one simple purpose. The wine press exerts controlled pressure in order to free the juice from the grape. Winemakers use caution when pressing to ensure that the seeds of the grapes do not burst. If the seeds burst, then they add an undesirable taste to the juice. Therefore, winemakers are very cautious when pressing. The more effective the pressing, the sweeter and better taste of the wine. The goal is to press the grapes to produce something greater in the long run.

When we are becoming, there will be times when the Lord will allow us to be wine pressed. In this sense, we are the grapes, and the Lord is the winemaker. Sometimes the Lord will take us through transitions that are pressing and uncomfortable. Like the winemaker, the Lord does not intend on bursting the core of who we are. In fact, the Lord allows us to be pressed enough so that He can extract from us something greater and sweeter. Whenever we find ourselves going through a pressing season, God is not trying to destroy us, He is trying to create us. The Lord is not trying to reduce us, He is in the transition of producing us. Sometimes God has to squeeze things out of us through trying, testing, and uncomfortable seasons. I want you to know that if you are in a pressing season, it simply means there is something greater within you that He wants to extract. **Philippians 3:14 |NIV| *"I press on toward the goal to win the prize for which God has called me heavenward in Christ Jesus."***

As a youth minister and a full-time graduate student with an internship, there are many moments when I feel pressed. Before I became a youth minster, I would only preach once a month as a guest speaker for other churches. Now that I am a youth minister, I am challenged with having to preach every week. At times, I find myself feeling the pressure of having to craft sermons on a weekly basis. There are moments when I feel fully prepared and there were times when I feel under-prepared. I was comfortable with having weeks in advance to prepare, but now I have a much shorter window of preparation. There are many high and low moments, good and bad days. I feel pressed and challenged on a much higher level now. I had to realize that God was pressing me. I reminded myself that this experience is not to punish me but to prepare me. Although there are times when I feel uncomfortable, it is meant to be that way. However, as time passed, I started to get more comfortable with prepping sermons in the weekly time span. What was outside of my norm had now become what is normal for me as I developed my ability to craft sermons effectively and efficiently.

Not only do I feel pressed with my youth ministry but also by my graduate course load. As a Master's student, the course curriculum challenges me in different ways. I am required to write many research papers that need to meet strenuous requirements in order to be considered for a grade. This requires me to conduct in depth research. I read more academic books than I have ever done in my life. Although I find myself pressed by the strenuous coursework, I also know that something greater is being extracted from me. My vocabulary and use of academic terminologies in my field of study has begun to expand. Not only is that true on paper but also in my speech. As a Master's level student, I find myself surrounded by a diverse cohort of colleagues of different ages and backgrounds. Being surrounded by academic scholars allows me to engage in scholarly dialogue and intellectually intriguing conversations. Being exposed to these academic settings made me realize I had to expand my vocabulary. Academic conversations are not necessarily about opinions but also facts and research. Although my graduate course load is pressing at times, I have extracted a new level of academic ability.

While being a youth minister, Master's student, and intern, I realized that each of these experiences had successfully extracted spiritual and academic growth and maturity from me. It is only by applying pressure through uncomfortable and pressing times that we extract the potential lying dormant within us. Each of these situations was uncomfortable, pressing, and pressuring. There were moments when I wondered if remaining steadfast was even worth the struggle. However, sometimes God puts us in new situations so that we can discover new versions of ourselves. Sometimes God will use experiences to push us so He can pull something greater out of us. By all means, this is not easy. God never promised it would be. But it is what will be extracted in the future that makes it worthwhile.

Maybe God has called you to a wine pressing season in your life. Maybe God has called you to lead a Bible study or volunteer at your church and you've never done it before. Maybe God has called you to a new position, internship, or job. When we are in the beginning of a new transition, it may feel strenuous and uncomfortable. However, if we do not give up, but remain persistent and consistent, it will become more natural over time.

Think of the challenge as one who is beginning to lift weights. A person who is a beginner in weight lifting does not start off by lifting a massive amount of weight. Instead, they start off with lighter weights. Given the fact that the person is new to lifting weights, their muscles will not be accustomed to the tension and strain of weight lifting, and they will become sore. Over time, the more they continue to lift weights, the more their muscles will adapt to the tension and strain. Through consistency and persistence, they will be able to lift more weight because their body has adapted and has been transformed through what was uncomfortable and pressing. In the same sense, sometimes God will ask us to lift something new in our lives. Because we have never lifted it before we may find ourselves feeling sore, strained, and uncomfortable. Just as a trainer gives the trainee enough weight to not be overwhelming, God does the same to us. The Lord will give us just enough to where it feels strenuous and uncomfortable, but He will never give us more than we are capable of lifting. **1 Corinthians 10:13 |NIV| "And God is faithful. He will not allow the temptation to be more than you can stand."**

Therefore, there are times in our becoming when we must press like never before. There will be times when we feel like giving up. But we must press forward and push ourselves to the mountain top even when it gets hard. There were times I had to press myself forward through the challenges of writing sermons every week. There were times I had to press myself through the coursework of my Master's program. No matter what, keep pressing forward. Do not give up.

One day when Jesus was passing through a town, he met a woman who was suffering. **Mark 5:25-26 |NLT| "A woman in the crowd had suffered for twelve years with constant bleeding. She had suffered a great deal from many doctors, and over the years she had spent everything she had to pay them, but she had gotten no better. In fact, she had gotten worse."** Although the woman found herself in a pressing situation, she had one goal in mind. She believed that if she touched the robe of Jesus then she would be healed. But a large crowd around Jesus was blocking her pathway to Him. **Mark 5:31 |NLT| "His disciples said to him, "Look at this crowd pressing around you."** But the woman managed to push through to Jesus. She then touched the robe of Jesus and instantly her bleeding stopped. **Mark 5:28-29 |NLT|** *"For she thought to herself, "If I can just touch his robe, I will be healed." Immediately the bleeding stopped, and she could feel in her body that she had been healed of her terrible condition."*

The woman was in a pressing moment, but this woman remained resolute in touching the robe of Jesus. I'm encouraging you to be like this woman. Just as the robe of Jesus was the woman's goal, whatever your goal is, you can touch it as well. Press through college so that you can touch that college degree. Press through your storm because weeping may endure for a night but your joy shall cometh in the morning. Press through the path in order to reach the mountain top of your dream. Press through the process to reach the promise God has for your life. Press through long days and early mornings because it will all be worth it soon. Press through hard times because better days are ahead. Press through that internship because it is only sharpening your craft and making you more credible and qualified for the future that is to come. Whatever your finish line is, press through.

When was a time in your life when you felt like you were being wine pressed? When did you feel like you were experiencing a pressing situation? When was a time in your life when you felt as though God allowed you to be pressed in order to extract something better from you in the long run? What in your life has pressed you by challenging you through situations that pushed you outside your comfort zone? What was extracted from you? What did you learn from these pressing times? How will you press through wine pressing seasons in your life?

_____

_____

. . .

The Transition of Becoming

12

The Transition of: The Dark Room
ANOINTED BUT NOT APPOINTED

Anointed means to choose by or as if by divine election, while appointed means to be assigned to a task or a position[1].

I want you to know that you are anointed. That if you are reading these words, it is not by chance, coincidence, nor accident. This moment is by divine providence. God has called you for something and has placed a goal or vision within you that is meant to happen. I believe you are anointed for ministry, you are anointed for motivational speaking, and you are anointed for entrepreneurship. However, God has an appointed time when He plans to bless, elevate, or take us to new heights and new levels.

Sometimes we may find ourselves feeling anointed for something but not appointed in the moment. We may find ourselves anointed to have a thriving business, but it may not be appointed to blossom until a later time. Sometimes we may find ourselves anointed with a talent, but it may not be appointed to reach a stage until a later time. You may feel anointed for the job of your dreams after you graduate from school, but you may not be appointed until sometime later. It can be frustrating to know you have so much promise but no platform. It is challenging to know you have so much shine but no spotlight. We can know we have so much presence but no stage to be present on. This is what it means to be anointed but not appointed. You have to remember that greatness and success may not happen overnight.

It did not happen overnight for David. After David was anointed king by the prophet Samuel, he did not ascend to his throne. **1 Samuel 16:13 |NLT| *"So as David stood there among his brothers, Samuel took the flask of olive oil he had brought and anointed David with the oil. And the Spirit of the Lord came powerfully upon David from that day on. Then Samuel returned to Ramah."*** In fact, Samuel returned to the land he came from, and David went back to tending his sheep.

Understand, if you feel anointed but not yet appointed, it is for divine reasons. It means you are experiencing what I call "the dark room." Camera film is purposely hidden from the spotlight because it is only in the dark room that the photos are able to develop and reach their full quality. Camera film photos are not meant to be exposed to light too soon because the photos must develop in the dark room first. If the camera film pictures are exposed to the light before being taken to the dark room then it can result in the photos not developing to their best quality.

In the same sense, God will sometimes take us into a dark room so that we can develop. Many of us want to run into the spotlight, but God does not want us exposed too soon simply because He wants us to develop to our full potential. If we are exposed to the blessing, promotion, or what we prayed for too soon it can backfire. We truly develop only in the dark room. Don't worry about being seen, focus on developing. **James 1:4 |NIV| *"Let perseverance finish its work so that you may be mature and complete, not lacking anything."*** After David was anointed king, he went through the transition of a dark room.

Once David was anointed king, the spirit of the Lord left Saul. Saul became tormented by a spirit of fear and depression.

1 Samuel 16:14 |NLT| *"Now the Spirit of the Lord had left Saul, and the Lord sent a tormenting spirit that filled him with depression and fear."* Saul's servants advised him to seek out a musician to play music and help him cope with the tormenting spirit. **1 Samuel 16:15-16 |NLT|** *"Some of Saul's servants said to him, "A tormenting spirit from God is troubling you. Let us find a good musician to play the harp whenever the tormenting spirit troubles you. He will play soothing music, and you will soon be well again."* Saul's servants found out that David was a skilled harpist. David was sent to Saul and began to serve him. **1 Samuel 16:21 |NLT|** *"So David went to Saul and began serving him. Saul loved David very much, and David became his armor bearer."* **1 Samuel 16:23 |NLT|** *"And whenever the tormenting spirit from God troubled Saul, David would play the harp. Then Saul would feel better, and the tormenting spirit would go away."*

David, the newly appointed King of Israel had been anointed for the crown but had not been appointed to the throne. Instead, he transitioned to a dark room. In fact, while David was in Saul's court no one knew he was the newly anointed king. They just thought of him as a shepherd boy who played the harp well. David was anointed for the spotlight, but he had not been appointed to the light. David was in the presence of greats who were unaware that he, too, was great. David was in the presence of a king who did not know that he also had a crown. David was in a dark room simply because he was in a position where his full potential was hidden from the spotlight. Nobody could see his full quality and who God had called him to be. Many of us also find ourselves in this same position. Maybe you feel as though your full quality is being hidden. Maybe people do not see your potential as an intern in a big-time company or business. Maybe you feel as though you have talent, but you are underestimated or overlooked. Maybe you feel as though you are in the presence of greats who do not know you are also great.

The Transition of Becoming

The transition of the dark room may feel like we are being hidden, but we are actually being covered by the divine timing of the Lord. The Lord was allowing David to develop by having him next to the throne that would soon be his. If David had ascended as soon as he was anointed, he may not have been ready to be the king. In the same way, God gives us blessings at appointed times because if we receive the blessings too early we may not be ready for them. Remember, there are levels to the process of becoming. Sometimes before we ascend we have to first attend. Sometimes in order to be over something, we first have to be of it. Sometimes before we are in the spotlight, we have to be a shadow. There was a moment in my life when I felt anointed but not appointed and that I had transitioned to a dark room.

One day, I received a phone call from a church. When I answered, the liaison stated, "Hey Minister Warren, we really like the positive things you are doing and would really love for you to come out and give a five-minute homily to our congregation for our Youth and College Sunday. And afterwards, we'd love if you could also sell copies of your book." The liaison then informed me that the church extending this invitation was New Birth Missionary Baptist Church. I was in a state of disbelief because New Birth Missionary Baptist Church is one of the largest and fastest growing churches in Georgia. I was excited because the pastor of this church is Jamal Bryant, who is a well-respected figure head in ministry. The liaison on the phone guaranteed this opportunity would grant me the chance to speak to a church of about 5,000 attendees and also meet Pastor Bryant. I would also have the opportunity to reach thousands with my book in one sitting.

After I graciously accepted the invitation, I pranced around my room, excited and still a little shocked since I did not kick down this door of opportunity. Instead, the door was brought to me already open and waiting on me to walk through. I dropped to my knees and thanked the Lord because I knew this opportunity could only have come from Him. Moments like this are the very things that I knew not to take for granted. Before this opportunity, I had spoken only to local churches. I had never had the opportunity of speaking to a mega church, but I always believed an opportunity like this would emerge and surely enough it did. However, what I thought was my time to be appointed to a grand stage would actually be my transition to the dark room.

Close to the date of the event, the liaison notified me that I would no longer be speaking to the church congregation due to scheduling conflicts. However, I was still extended an invitation to attend the service, meet Pastor Bryant, and sell some of my books to the congregation. Even though I would no longer be speaking, I still saw this as an amazing opportunity. I dressed in my favorite suit, dress shoes, and bow tie. I believe in the philosophy of, "You only get one first impression." I would not take this opportunity for granted. I knew that although I wasn't going to grace the stage, gracing the presence of the church was a blessing within itself.

Upon arriving at the church, I was escorted and seated in the pulpit area of the church. As I sat on the stage facing the large crowd of people, I thought to myself how amazing it would be to grace this stage in the name of the Lord. It was a bitter sweet moment. Although I was not speaking on the stage, I knew it was a matter of God's grace that I was seated on the stage. Suddenly, Pastor Jamal Bryant was escorted to his seat in the pulpit a few feet in front of me. Throughout the entire service, I wanted to humbly introduce myself to Pastor Bryant. Not only as an up-and-coming minister but as someone who respects his service to the community. However, I knew deep within my spirit this wasn't the right time. The Lord told my spirit to be patient and not rush anything. I was in the same space as someone I well respected who did not even know I was there, let alone that I even existed.

After the service ended, I expected to meet Jamal Bryant.

The Transition of Becoming

Instead of speaking to the congregation, I was asked to speak to the youth group, and there I was supposed to meet Pastor Bryant. I was taken to the youth room with about twenty-five high school and college students. As I waited to speak to the youth group, Jamal Bryant entered the youth room. However, a few moments before I was called up to speak to the youth group, he left the room. Although I was speaking to a small group of youth, I still spoke just as passionately as if I was speaking to the congregation.

After I finished speaking, three people approached me and found interest in my book. In this moment, I had experienced being anointed but not being appointed. I felt anointed with my passion and excitement knowing that I possessed the confidence to grace the stage, reach the audience with my book, and even meet Pastor Jamal. However, I did not feel appointed because none of these opportunities came true. I felt anointed for the stage but had been appointed to speak to a youth group. I felt anointed to reach the congregation with my book but had been appointed to reach a few youths. I felt anointed to meet Pastor Jamal but was not appointed with the opportunity to shake his hand. I felt like I was in a dark room.

When I got into my car, I put my head on the steering wheel. I felt a little disappointed in the outcome. Initially, I was offered the opportunity to speak to a congregation of 5,000 while also meeting Jamal Bryant and reaching the congregation with copies of my book. I saw this as a long-awaited opportunity and a chance to leave a trailblazing mark. I then looked out the window of my car and said, "God what was the point of this?" In that moment, I felt the Lord speak to my spirit. The Lord said, "I did this to show you that I did not bury you, but I have planted you. And I can sprout you at any moment." The Lord said, "I did it to show you that as quick as I can get you in the presence of greatness is as quick as I can elevate you to greatness." Sometimes

God will bring us appetizers before He brings out the full course meal to see if we will trust in Him. Sometimes the Lord will show us a preview to the sequel of blessings He has for us to see if we will just sit back and trust the next scene that He has written for our lives.

I realized that God can make anything happen on His timing. I had to reevaluate my emotions because this wasn't an opportunity for me to show my gifts, but for God to remind me that all my hard work is not in vain. The fact that I found myself at New Birth Missionary Baptist Church seated on the same stage as Jamal Bryant and speaking to a youth group after one phone call was a reflection of God's grace. Although the experience did not play out exactly how it was initially presented, I was reminded that God can take us from being anointed to being appointed at any moment. That any time we doubt or do not trust God, it can be an insult to His divine power. I realized that it simply wasn't time yet. God was letting me know He had not forgotten about everything He had shown me. It was a reminder that God does not bury us, He plants us.

Many of us think that when blessings do not sprout as quick as we hoped, that we are buried. In fact, it can be easy to think our dreams and aspirations have been buried when God actually planted them. A coffin and a seed both have the same burial process. The coffin requires digging up dirt, placing the coffin in the ground, and then putting the dirt back on top. The same process works for the seed. The difference is that one is meant to stay in the ground, and the other is meant to sprout and blossom from the ground. Sometimes God has to work underground in our lives. Even if you can't see God working, you have to know that He is. Although you may not see it, God is growing something in you, your dream, or vision that sprouts from strong roots. Sometimes the Lord has to start at the root. Any plant that does not have strong roots usually does not last. When God plants our visions and dreams, it may take time. When God plants us, the harvest may take longer than we anticipate. However, you have to know you are an anointed seed that has been planted, and you will sprout in God's appointed time.

Much like David as a harpist in Saul's court, I was in the presence of greats who did not know I was great. I saw myself in the midst of visionaries who did not know I also had a vision. In my case, it simply wasn't time to be sprouted. It simply was not time be appointed. Being reminded that God could appoint me at any moment inspired me to stay ready. This experience reminded me that any opportunity can present itself at any moment. And when the Lord says go, we cannot be trying to get ready. Instead, we should already be ready. I knew that the dark room was meant for my good and not for my harm. Therefore, this helped me understand the importance of perfecting my craft.

Have you ever felt anointed but not appointed? Have you ever felt like you were in the presence of greats who did not know you were great? Have you ever felt like you were in a dark room? Have you ever felt like God was developing you behind closed doors? When is a time in your life when you felt anointed and not appointed? When is a time in your life when you felt like you transitioned to the dark room?

_____

_____

_____

_____

_____

. . .

WARREN HAWKINS III

13

The Transition of: Preparation
PERFECTING THE PROPHETIC

Perfect means to make ready beforehand for some purpose, use, or activity. It can also mean to make (something) completely free from faults or defects, or as close to such a condition as possible. Prophetic is a prediction that accurately describes or predicts what will happen in the future[1].

"It is better to be prepared for an opportunity and not have one than to have an opportunity and not be prepared." —Whitney M. Young, Jr.

I want you to believe wholeheartedly that your craft, vision, and dream is prophetic. I want you to know that whatever God placed in your heart can come to pass. The question is, will you be ready for whatever you are asking? The big promotion you are asking God for; will you be ready for it if He gives it to you tomorrow? The speaking engagement you are praying for; will you be ready for it if He gives it to you in the next five minutes? Will you be ready to leave for the book tour if the Lord blessed you with one? Do you already have your next steps and goals organized? I want you to believe that whatever you want to become and do in this life is prophetic, which means it has the poten-

tial to come to pass in the future. But may I submit for your consideration that maybe God has not given you what you are praying for because you are not prepared.

We have to be willing to perfect what is prophetic for our lives. It's easy to want the prophetic promise but not want the prophetic preparation that it will take. It is easy to want a prophetic word but not want the prophetic work ethic that must come with it. We have to be willing to practice, prepare, and perfect what it is that we are working toward. Your dream, vision, and goals are prophetic. It is destined to happen. However, you have to be willing to perfect what it is you believe in. Perfect that business plan, your public speaking, your artwork, and your sales pitch. The Lord wants to give you the opportunity, but are you ready for the opportunity? The Lord wants to take you to the stage, but have you started to walk up the steps? The Lord wants to put you on the big screen, but have you taken the opportunity to get yourself together behind the scenes? If you know and believe that it will happen, then why aren't you preparing as if it is going to happen?

The problem is some of us are praying but not preparing. Think of it as a cook who plans to prepare a meal for a large group of guests. Logically, the cook should not wait until the guests arrive to start preparing. In fact, the cook should have already gotten the groceries from the store and cooked the meal before the guests arrive. If the guests arrive and the cook is still out gathering groceries and preparing the meal, then that would mean the cook is unprepared for what is to come. It is illogical to invite guests and not have food prepared. In the same sense, many of us ask God to send blessings and opportunities our way, but we have not taken the time to perfect and prepare for what we know and believe will arrive. Understand, preparation meets opportunity and what we perfect has the potential to become prophetic. As we continue to dissect the story of David, we learn that what he perfected led to something prophetic for his life.

One day a mighty Philistine warrior named Goliath challenged King Saul and the entire Israelite army. Goliath mocked and dared anyone from Israel to go against him in a one-on-one battle. **1 Samuel 17:8 |NLT|** ***"Goliath stood and shouted*** *a taunt across to the Israelites. "Why are you all coming out to fight?" he called. "I am the Philistine champion, but you are only the servants of Saul. Choose one man to come down here and fight me!"* None of the men from Israel had the courage to step up and fight Goliath due to his might and overwhelming appearance. **1 Samuel 17:4-6 |NLT|** *"Then Goliath, a Philistine champion from Gath, came out of the Philistine ranks to face the forces of Israel. He was over nine feet tall! He wore a bronze helmet, and his bronze coat of mail weighed 125 pounds. He also wore bronze leg armor, and he carried a bronze javelin on his shoulder."* The only person who was willing to accept the challenge was David.

1 Samuel 17:32 |NLT| *"Don't worry about this Philistine," David told Saul. "I'll go fight him!"* When David said this, Saul insisted that David was incapable of defeating Goliath. Saul told David he was only a shepherd boy and stood no chance against Goliath. In fact, this was true. At the time, David was only a shepherd and an attendant to Saul. He was not a warrior and had no war experience. However, David insisted he could take Goliath down because he had perfected a secret craft. **1 Samuel 17:34-36 |NLT|** *"But David persisted. "I have been taking care of my father's sheep and goats," he said. "When a lion or a bear comes to steal a lamb from the flock, I go after it with a club and rescue the lamb from its mouth. If the animal turns on me, I catch it by the jaw and club it to death. I have done this to both lions and bears, and I'll do it to this pagan Philistine, too, for he has defied the armies of the living God!"*

David promised that as a shepherd he had to defend and protect his sheep from lions and bears with a sling shot. He insisted he had perfected the art of the slingshot, and he was confident because of what he had perfected, which had led him to this prophetic moment. He did not see Goliath as opposition but rather as an opportunity. He did not see Goliath as a problem but rather as a platform. David knew he wouldn't miss with all of Israel watching because he had perfected his craft when no one was watching. He knew he could slay a giant in public because he had perfected slaying giants in private. David was able to do this because he saw his pasture as preparation for a prophetic opportunity. Therefore, he knew he would not miss in this opportunity because he was already prepared for it.

Understand, Goliath was not slain in the moment he was slain. Goliath was already slain in the moments when David perfected his craft. I want you to believe that your opportunity is not achieved once you achieve it. Your opportunity is achieved the moment you prepare for it. If you see yourself on the screen, you have to be willing to perfect your monologues and scripts. If you want to be promoted in your job or business, you have to be willing to perfect your pitch. If you see yourself owning that business, you have to be willing to perfect the outline of a plan. If you see your book, vision, or brand reaching many people, then you have to perfect reaching those around you first. Because David had perfected what seemed small, he was qualified for something bigger. Your craft may start off small, but if we take the time to prefect what seems small God may promote us to something bigger. God wants the prophetic to happen in your life, but you have to be willing to prepare for it.

One day I was invited as a keynote speaker for a back-to-school rally for middle and high school students. I was excited and elated to be a keynote speaker. I prepared what I believed to be an impactful message. But when the day of the event arrived not one youth was in attendance. The only people there were the event hosts and organizers. The event organizers and coordinators were disappointed with the outcome. However, I had a different mindset. I did not see this as wasted time. I saw this as an opportunity to perfect and practice my craft and to empower and encourage the event organizers.

As the event host prepared to give his farewell remarks, I raised my hand and asked if I could speak. I began to encourage the group. I told them that instead of feeling like they had many reasons to look down, they had every reason to look up. I told them that, "God sometimes does not honor us based on the outcome of what we produce, but He honors us based on our willingness to still produce without knowing the outcome." I also told them their willingness to be obedient and host the event was a reflection of their hearts. This was a humbling moment for me because not only was I speaking to them, but I was speaking to myself. I was not only reminding them to keep pushing for the promise even in times of discouragement, I was also reminding myself to do the same.

At times, churches turned me down for opportunities to speak. I shed tears just wanting an opportunity to walk in the promise God had for my life. But even while looking in the face of rejection, I kept on writing sermons and preparing as if I was booked to preach that following Sunday. There would be other times when I wanted my book to reach many people. However, I had to learn to perfect reaching those around me first. I made creative flyers and videos that advertised my book on social media. I also reached out to close friends and family members. I received a great deal of help from my father. My father would purchase a large number of my books and encourage his co-workers to purchase a copy. At times I had to ride the Greyhound bus to travel to my speaking engagements. I would arrive at churches where I was scheduled to speak and only a few people would be in the room. Regardless of how many people were in attendance, I still gave it my all as if the seats were filled.

As a young minister with future ministry aspirations, there were times in my college dorm room when I preached sermons and recited poems to the walls, and these walls became as transparent as glass. I would close my eyes and see all the promise I believed God had for my life. These were times when I decided to perfect the prophetic for my life. I remind myself every day to keep preparing and practicing for what I desire. When the day comes, I won't have to get ready because I'll already be ready.

Here I am like David, conquering lions and bears just as I am conquering speaking to local crowds and reaching those around me with my book. Here I am like David in my pasture, waiting for my prophetic opportunity. Here I am like David, perfecting my sling shot so that I can have my big shot. As long as we stay prepared, God will allow us to attract whatever we extract. Instead of us having to find the platform, the platform will find us. Instead of us searching for the opportunity, the opportunity will seek us.

David did not go out and seek Goliath. In fact, Goliath sought after David, demanding a warrior from the Israelite army. David did not have to create the opportunity; the opportunity was created for him. In the same way, when we are prepared and perfected in our craft, we won't have to go looking for the opportunity. The opportunity will be waiting on us. When we perfect our craft, God will have a prophetic blessing that has our name on it. In fact, Goliath taunted all the Israelites for forty days and no one from Saul's army stepped up. **1 Samuel 17:16 |NLT| "For forty days, every morning and evening, the Philistine champion strutted in front of the Israelite army."** *No one stepped up because this opportunity was David's prophetic moment and promise. And once David arrived, it was he who qualified for the blessing. God has aligned opportunity, promotion, and blessings for which only you are qualified. God wants to lead you to doors that only you will be given the keys to. You are not in competition with anyone other than yourself for what is prophetic for your life.*

As David and Goliath prepared to battle, Saul attempted to give David his own armor but he refused. **1 Samuel 17:38-39 |NLT| "Then Saul gave David his own armor—a bronze helmet and a coat of mail. David put it on, strapped the sword over it, and took a step or two to see what it was like, for he had never worn such things before. "I can't go in these," he protested to Saul. "I'm not used to them." So David took them off."** *David did not need to rely on Saul's armor because He was confident not only in his abilities but God's favor.* **1 Samuel 37:45-46 |NLT| "David replied to the Philistine, "You come to** me with sword, spear, and javelin, but I come to you in the name of the Lord of Heaven's Armies—the God of the armies of Israel, whom you have defied. Today the Lord will conquer you."* In the same sense, when we have true faith in our abilities and God's promises, there is no need to rely on the hand outs and connections of other people. Instead of focusing on impressing people and shaking the next hand, we should focus on bettering our craft and skills. Promotion does not come from man or woman but from God. There's a saying, "who you know can get you in the door, but what you know will keep you in the room." In David's case, his favor with God got him in the door of this opportunity, but his ability to perfect his sling shot kept him in the room.

1 Samuel 17:48-50 |NLT| *"As Goliath moved closer to attack, David quickly ran out to meet him. Reaching into his shepherd's bag and taking out a stone, he hurled it with his sling and hit the Philistine in the forehead. The stone sank in, and Goliath stumbled and fell face down on the ground. So David triumphed over the Philistine with only a sling and a stone."* After David defeated Goliath, Saul made David the commander of his army. **1 Samuel 18:5 |NLT| *"Whatever Saul asked David to do, David did it successfully. So Saul made him a commander over the men of war, an appointment that was welcomed by the people and Saul's officers alike."***

Because David perfected his craft, it led to a prophetic opportunity for his life. Again, I tell you that your craft, dream, vision, and pasture is prophetic. It has the potential to lead to the promise for your life. David's craft was a sling shot he perfected that led to a prophetic shot and an opportunity to change his life. It was the pasture that prepared him for the promise. Just as David did, we must prefect our craft. Don't underestimate this time in your pasture, use it to prepare for the promise. If you know you have a big vision and a big dream, prepare and prefect your craft now so that you will be ready when the moment comes.

David did not have to practice after Goliath came because he had already perfected his craft. In the same sense, we must prefect our craft not after the blessing, promotion, or opportunity comes but before it comes. If we stay ready we will not have to get ready. David knew all he needed was one shot because he treated the pasture like it was his one shot. He was ready when God finally gave him his SHOT. So don't you dare sleep in your pasture or give up on your process. Keep perfecting your craft and continue to work on your sling shot. When God takes you from process to promise, you had better be ready because all of Israel will be watching. The whole world will be a witness, and people who can take you higher in your calling and your purpose will be in the room.

You can't flinch, you can't hesitate. You have to be ready. So get ready, because the prophetic for your life is coming soon.

What do you believe is the prophetic for your life? How will you perfect the prophetic for your life? What are the opportunities you are praying for? How will you prepare for the very opportunities you are asking for? What is the big moment or opportunity you are awaiting? How will you use the content of this chapter to help you perfect the prophetic for your life?

_____

_____

_____

_____

_____

. . .

The Transition of Becoming

14

The Transition of: Multipurposed Responsibility
PROTECT, ATTEND, ASCEND

Multipurposed means having several purposes or functions or being able to serve more than one purpose. Responsibility is a duty or obligation to satisfactorily perform or complete a task[1].

"You take on the responsibility of making your dream a reality"—Les Brown

Have you ever felt like you did not have the energy to pursue your dream because you had other responsibilities pulling at your energy? Have you ever spent entire days giving to everything and everyone else, but when it was time to give to yourself you had nothing left to give? Have you ever spent so much time pouring into everything and everybody else that when it was time to pour into yourself, your cup was empty? Have you ever felt like there weren't enough hours in the day to put you first? Have you ever felt like your day was divided amongst different responsibilities? Have you ever felt like you didn't have the energy to do what you wanted to do because you were consumed with the things you had to do. If so, you are in a transition of multipurposed responsibility.

Multipurposed responsibility is when we have multiple priorities that each serve different functions in our life. Maybe you have the responsibility of going to college and working a job while still trying to pursue your dreams and aspirations. Maybe you are a parent and have the responsibility of working jobs while parenting your children. Maybe you stepped back from your dream so that your offspring could step up to theirs. Maybe instead of driving to the destination of your dream, you took a detour down roads for the dreams of your children. Maybe you feel as though your time to pursue and become what you desired has passed. Maybe you feel as though it continuously passes by simply because you are always consumed with other demanding responsibilities.

Yes, you have a responsibility to your job, your family, and your finances, but I also want to remind you that you have a responsibility to becoming everything God predestined you to become. It is also your responsibility to achieve the desires He has placed in your heart. I want you to know that having multipurposed responsibility is challenging, but it is not impossible to manage. It only seems impossible because you have put limitations on your mind. Don't give up on your dream just because you may have to work long hours. I know you may be drained, tired, and exhausted, but please don't give up. I want you to believe again. I want you to get your fire and vision back. Don't you dare limit yourself nor let excuses create limitations on your life. Someone took the same or similar situation and won with it. Someone took your same excuses and exchanged them for opportunity. In the transition of multipurposed responsibility, it is possible for us to balance our responsibilities. Sometimes we will have to balance three responsibilities: to protect, attend, and ascend.

As we explored the story of David, we came to know that he also went through the transition of multipurposed responsibility. At one point, David was a shepherd, servant to Saul, and an anointed and not yet appointed king. **1 Samuel 17:14-15**

|NLT| *"David was the youngest son. David's three oldest brothers stayed with Saul's army, but David went back and forth so he could help his father with the sheep in Bethlehem."* David was faced with the multipurposed responsibility to protect and attend, while waiting to ascend. David had to protect his sheep from lions and bears. He also had to attend, by being an attendant to King Saul in his court. Lastly, David had the responsibility of soon ascending to his promised throne as King of Israel.

Much like David, sometimes we will be faced with multipurposed responsibilities. David had the responsibility of protecting his sheep as a shepherd. In the same way, we have sheep we must protect in the form of our dream, vision, or goals. Anytime lions or bears tried to harm David's sheep, He defended his sheep using a sling shot. By all means, David protected his sheep. We must have this same mindset in our lives and not let anything harm our sheep. We have to be willing to protect what we want to become. And sometimes the battle is within ourselves. Doubt, discouragement, and fatigue may try to harm our dreams and aspirations, but we must be willing to defend our dreams. Protect your idea, protect your business, and your goals. You may have aspirations to graduate from college, be sure to protect yourself from moments of wanting to give up. Your sheep may be your dreams. You have to protect your dreams from any type of negativity that will cause you to falter. Speak light and not night and speak life and not death. Speak positivity and not negativity over your life. **Proverbs 18:21 |NKJV|** *"Death and life are in the power of the tongue: and they that love it shall eat the fruit thereof."*

Your sheep may be your own self love and confidence. You have to protect yourself from relationships and people who may take advantage of you. Be sure to protect your heart and protect yourself. Be unapologetic about who you allow into your space and your heart. **Proverbs 4:23 |NIV|** *"Above all else,* *guard your heart, for everything you do flows from it."* Your sheep may be your purity. Be sure to protect it from those who may try to snatch away your mission to maintain a life of purity. Be sure to protect yourself from people who may try to seduce or deceive you from becoming the one in your family who remained committed to staying pure. Look at the story of David, he did not let a lion or bear come close to harming his sheep. David knew the moment he let lions and bears close to his sheep it would lead to his sheep being devoured. Therefore, you cannot let some people close to you simply because they have the potential to devour what it is that you have vowed to protect. **1 Corinthians 15:33 |NIV| *Do not be misled: "Bad company corrupts good character."***

You may be a parent and the sheep you need to protect may be your children. You have to be willing to protect your children from negative influences, distractions, unhealthy relationships, and anything that is going to devour their becoming. As a parent, it is your responsibility to protect the becoming of your child. In fact, my mother always says, "Parenting does not end when a child turns eighteen or goes off to college." That's when parenting truly begins simply because the age eighteen is only a new beginning to who they will become for the rest of their lives. Once young people transition into the next stage in life, that's when everything they have learned or been taught will be put to the test. When young people transition to high school or college, or even out of the home, that is when new portals of decisions and self-discovery will open. So, parents, you have a responsibility to protect your child. **Proverbs 22:6 |NKJV| *"Train up a child in the way he should go, and when he is old he will not depart from it."*** Parenting is not a nine to five job, meaning there are no breaks, vacations, nor retirements. Regardless of how old someone's child may get, they are still that person's child, so continue to train them and point them in the right direction no matter how old they become. David did not let lions or bears get close to his sheep. Parents, I ask, are you letting negative influences, distractions, and toxic relationships get close to your children? You must be willing to protect your children through your words, actions, and continual guidance.

Even while being a college student, my mother and father still use their words and conversations as a shield for protecting my becoming. My parents are not just nurturers and providers, but they are also life coaches. There are moments when they take control of the wheel of my life to steer me in the right direction. But there are also moments when they let me take the wheel so I can experience some paths for myself. However, they never let me take roads alone. They sometimes will take the passenger seat and point me in the direction I should be going. The words of my parents echo in my consciousness and guide me through everyday life decisions. I may not get it right all the time, but I always have their words and support as a reference and guide to my life. There are times when they will alert me to a stumbling block ahead, and sometimes I do not take heed to their warnings, and it results in me stumbling. However, their hand is always stretched out to help me back on my feet whenever I may fall.

My parents' words are not just in me, but they are a part of me and are a part of who I am becoming. Without the guidance of my parents, I would not be in the transition of becoming who I am today. For instance, after graduating with my Bachelor's degree, my parents encouraged me to go beyond. They reminded me that the sky is not the limit. They reminded me to never settle for the things I can see, but to go beyond. I am now a Master's student, and after I obtain my Master's, I will go beyond in my academic pursuits. Overall, because of my parents' words of protection, I am on the path to becoming a product of parents who verbally protect their child.

Whatever it is in your life that needs protecting, then by all means necessary, protect it. While protecting our sheep, we must also be willing to tend to our priorities and responsibilities. David was given the responsibility of attending to Saul in his court. David had to tend to Saul by playing the harp. In a sense, David was an intern in Saul's court. In the same way, we may find ourselves having the responsibility of being an intern or working under someone else. That is okay, sometimes we have to first work under so that we can one day know how to work over. Sometimes we have to be the tail so we can one day be the head. Sometimes we have to be willing to help make someone else's dreams come true so that we can understand how to also make our dreams a reality. We can only imagine how much humility it took for David to serve Saul while knowing he had what it takes to be the King of Israel. In the same way, it is going to take you having humility to serve your boss while knowing you have what it takes to run the company. This is exactly what happened to David. David not only had to attend, but he knew that he would one day ascend to the throne of the prophetic promise for his life. David was able to protect his sheep and attend to Saul while waiting to ascend to his throne. David was multipurposed in his responsibility.

In addition, we must also be able to attend to our responsibilities of work, internship, education, relationships, and family while knowing and believing that God will allow us to ascend to new heights and new levels of the promise He has for our lives. This can be immensely disheartening and discouraging but we have to push through. Do not ponder on how things look, remain focused on what God said. Keep protecting the dream God placed in your heart. We also may feel undervalued, overlooked, and unappreciated. I understand, being an intern may not be praiseworthy. Being a college student with a strenuous course load may be underappreciated. Working at jobs and taking care of a family may be draining. There may be times when we feel unenthused, unmotivated, and drained. However, we cannot give up. Better days are ahead. The pasture is temporary and what we are tending to, we will soon ascend from. I am currently going through my own transition of multipurposed responsibility where I have to protect, attend, while wholeheartedly believing that I will one day ascend.

Currently as a youth minister, a full-time graduate student, and an intern, I find myself in a transition of multipurposed responsibility. I find myself tending to multiple responsibilities at once. There are moments when I am working on sermons, research papers, and therapeutic group facilitation lessons at the same time. There are many times when I find myself going back and forth to attend to multiple responsibilities. There are many times when I feel the pressure of having to prepare a message for my Sunday youth service. Many times, I feel like there are not enough hours in the day. There are days when I go to my internship from 9am to 5pm and then have graduate classes that evening with course work and other assignments due. I have to truly prioritize my time, and I have to become selective on what I attend to. I cannot get complacent with my time by attending to things that are distractions. Therefore, as a youth minister, intern, and full- time graduate student I spend most of my time preparing for Sundays, preparing to be a successful intern in my field placement, and studying and working on class assignments so that I can become a successful student.

As I wrote the manuscript for this book, I was also in the transition of multipurposed responsibility. I wrote this book while still having the other responsibilities of being a youth minister, intern, and student. Sometimes when we attend to a dream, we have to be willing to make sacrifices. There were many times when I would arise before sunrise and go to bed well after the sun had set. Many mornings before reporting to class or internship, I would read over the manuscript for this book. After long nights of writing research papers, I would stay up a few hours more to work on my manuscript. During this time, I realized I needed to tend to my financial stability. I decided to work for Door Dash, which is a food delivery service. There were many days when I would get off internship, finish preaching on Sunday, or get out of class and dedicate a few hours of my day to delivering food across town. I experienced many moments where I felt drained, exhausted, and unenthused.

Because I was attending to multiple responsibilities at once, I knew I had to protect my consciousness from subconscious thoughts that posed a threat to my positivity and confidence. At times when writing research papers, I would close my laptop out of frustration. I would then pep talk myself and soon open my laptop and get back to work. There were mornings when I did not feel motivated to preach. I had to protect myself through prayer in order to get through the morning. There were times when internship challenged me. However, I knew that if I kept tending to my responsibilities, they would ascend to something rewarding in the near future. Currently I am protecting myself from discouragement, tending to my responsibilities, while waiting to ascend to the next transition the Lord has for my life.

David's faithful protection of his sheep and tending to his responsibility in Saul's court resulted in him ascending to the throne as king. The transition of multipurposed responsibility can be discouraging and challenging. However, as long as we remain faithful to protecting and attending we will soon have the pleasure of ascending. Years can pass us by simply because we become overloaded with the responsibility of everything else in our lives. Regardless of how busy you are and how many responsibilities you have, you also have the responsibility of ascending to your dream. Sometimes dreams don't work unless we are willing to work. I use the method below to help me balance my responsibilities while also tending to my goals and dreams.

Start Yesterday

Many of us wonder when we should start something. When should we start writing the book? When should we start the business? When should we start our speaking career? When should we start pursuing higher education? The perfect time to start was yesterday. The more we ask ourselves this question, the more time passes. And if you know for a fact that God placed the dream in your heart, it is not meant to rot but to sprout into existence. If you never start the race then you will never make it to the finish line. Procrastination is the enemy of success, and fear is the thief of our futures. Doubt is the unfriendly neighbor of belief. When something is truly important to you, then you must find a way and not an excuse.

What are you waiting for? START YESTERDAY!! Start outlining that business plan, start applying to colleges, start pursuing speaking engagements, start your acting career. Start rehearsing those monologues, start getting your sales pitch together, start what it is that you desire! You think you are waiting on your destiny when your destiny is waiting on you. I am a firm believer that sometimes opportunities don't come to those who wait, sometimes opportunities come to those who are willing to create the opportunities. So, start making it happen!

Even God had to make it happen when He created the world. **Genesis 1:1-3 |NLT| *"In the beginning God created the heavens and the earth. The earth was formless and empty, and darkness covered the deep waters. And the Spirit of God was hovering over the surface of the waters. Then God said, "Let there be light," and there was light."*** *This scripture suggests the earth was void and formless, and there was nothing but darkness. The Lord did not sit around and ask Himself, "when should I start creating the Earth?" or "When is a perfect time to start?" No! Instead, He got right to work. If the Lord had never started then you and I would not be here today. So I ask, what is missing today because you have not started creating? And if God Himself had to start creating the world, then what makes us think we are exempted from starting and creating something for our lives. If we are not willing to take a risk for what's extraordinary, then we will settle for the ordinary.*

Push Yourself

Once you start pursuing and managing your dream, you will have to push yourself! There are no short cuts or cheat codes to hard work. Your dream is not going to pull itself toward you, so you have to push yourself toward it. It won't be easy, but you have to believe it's worth it. There will be many long nights and early mornings. **You must not treat your dream like a side hustle but as a means of survival.** *By any means necessary do not starve your dream. By any means necessary, make it happen. Even if you're tired, do it tired. Even if you're exhausted, do it exhausted. Regard-*

less, you are going to be tired. You can choose to be tired unfulfilled or either tired fulfilled. The choice is yours!

Pace Yourself

There are only two options, either to make progress or to make excuses. Therefore, sometimes in order to make progress for ourselves we must set goals that pace our pursuit. The purpose of a pace is to not to accelerate too much, or it can result in quick exhaustion. At the same time, moving at a set pace ensures that we do not fall behind in the race. Therefore, a pace is a steady speed toward a specific goal. I encourage you to pace yourself toward your goals. Do not move too fast or you will burn yourself out, but do not move too slow and fall behind.

Even the Lord set a pace when He created the world. God created the earth in six days. The Lord created specific things on the earth and in the universe on each day. The Bible clearly states that the Lord did not create the earth all in one day so we should not strive to make it all happen in one day. If the Lord paced Himself, then what makes us think we should not do the same. In fact, after the six days of creation, the Lord rested on the seventh day. **Genesis 2:1-2 |NLT| "So the creation of the heavens and the earth and everything in them was completed. On the seventh day God had finished his work of creation, so he rested from all his work."**

Therefore, some days are not meant to create but to rest. You do not have to do it all in one day and remember to rest. Remember to move at a steady pace. Just as the Lord moved at a steady pace by creating specific things for the world on each day, we can do the same. Set a pace for yourself. You can outline dates and deadlines for how you want to reach your goals and stay committed.

Have you ever transitioned to a season of multipurposed responsibility? Have you ever had to protect your dream while tending to a responsibility and trying to muster up the belief that you would soon ascend? How will you use what was discussed in this chapter to help you balance your responsibilities while going after your dream?

_____

_____

_____

_____

_____

_____

_____

_____

15

The Transition of: The Dry Valley
JUST KEEP DIGGING

A dry valley is cut by water erosion but contains no permanent surface stream. Dry valleys typically occur in an area of porous rock, such as limestone[1].

Finding Nemo is an American computer-animated film produced by Pixar. In the movie, a clown fish named Marlin ends up losing his son Nemo in the depths of the ocean. Marlin embarks on a relentless quest to find his missing son. During his quest, he meets another fish named Dory, and she decides to join him in his pursuit. When Marlin became discouraged and fatigued from the overwhelming pursuit, Dory gave him some advice. Dory told Marlin, "Just keep swimming! Just keep swimming! Just keep swimming, swimming, swimming!" She said these words in a jingle which made it sound like a song. Although an animated film, we can still take away a valuable lesson. Marlin wanted to find his son Nemo, and in order to find him he needed to keep swimming. We must apply this same mindset to our lives. Never give up, and keep going after what you want.

Have you ever felt like certain doors you humbly knocked on have yet to open? Have you ever felt like certain stars of opportunities you see from afar have not been given to you up close? Have you ever felt like the No's in your life have still not become Yes's. Have you ever felt like your seeds of ideas have yet to sprout? If so, this means you may have transitioned into a dry valley season in your life. There comes a time in each of our lives when we may experience a dry valley. A dry valley is land that does not sustain water flow. When we are in a dry valley in our lives it is up to us whether our valley remains dry or becomes nourished in blessings and overflow. Anytime we reach a dry valley, it is not a sign to falter in our faith. It is a reminder to finish the work. Anytime we face a dry valley, we must remember to "just keep digging."

The Bible talks about a time when the people of Israel were in a serious drought and there was no sign of rain. **2 Kings 3:9 |NLT| "And all three armies traveled along a roundabout route through the wilderness for seven days. But there was no water for the men or their animals."** The Israelites grew distraught and began to panic. **2 Kings 3:10 |NLT| "What should we do?" the king of Israel cried out. "The Lord has brought the three of us here to let the king of Moab defeat us."**

The Israelites were in a wilderness where they became distraught. They were preparing for war and needed water for themselves and their livestock. They had reached a dry valley, and they began to think it was time to give up. The Israelites were losing confidence in the battle all because the situation looked dry. And that's how some of us approach our lives. Many of us may feel like we are in a season when our seeds of visions, goals, and dreams are not getting any nourishment. We think that just because things get dry, it is time to give up. We think that just because we are not getting the results we hoped for, it is time to be negative and defeated. In fact, it is the exact opposite. The real work begins when we get tired. Just when it looks like nothing will happen for us, we have to be willing to make things happen. When things aren't going our way, we have to make things move in our favor. Anytime we reach a dry valley, it is not a sign for us to falter in our faith, but is a reminder to finish what we started.

The Transition of Becoming

The prophet Elisha spoke on behalf of God and instructed the Israelites on what they needed to do. **2 Kings 3:16-18 |NIV|** *"He then said, "God's word: Dig ditches all over this valley. Here's what will happen—you won't hear the wind, you won't see the rain, but this valley is going to fill up with water and your army and your animals will drink their fill. This is easy for God to do; he will also hand over Moab to you.* **2 Kings 3:20 |NIV|** *"In the morning—it was at the hour of morning sacrifice—the water had arrived, water pouring in from the west, from Edom, a flash flood filling the valley with water."*

God promised the Israelites the blessing of overflow. He promised to send the water they needed to survive. God also instructed them to dig holes to prepare for what was soon to come. And the following morning, water filled and nourished the dry valley. The same works in our lives when we find ourselves in a dry valley. Even if things look dry, deserted, and hopeless, God still wants us to keep digging for our dreams, goals, and the things we pray for. God will send the overflow. The question is, are you willing to dig for what it is that you are asking for? Are you willing to dig for the very thing that you want? Sometimes God moves after we prove we are willing to move. God will send the overflow once you start digging. You say that you are waiting on God, but maybe God is waiting on you. Maybe those doors remained closed in your life because God wants you to kick the door down. Maybe the star remains from afar because God wants you to reach for it. Maybe you were told No because you are meant to go out and create your own Yes. Maybe the seed of ideas has not sprouted simply because you have not taken the action to water it yourself. Understand, faith without works is dead.

There were many moments when I had to create opportunities for myself, fearfully laugh in the face of fear, and pep talk myself out of self-doubt. Many weapons formed, Yes's became No's, and doors closed in my face. Nevertheless, I couldn't let those same weapons prosper. I created my own Yes's, and I've kicked down doors in order to walk into the opportunities God ordained for my life. After releasing my first book *Shaped for Greater Works*, I felt as though I had reached a dry valley. I had worked very hard to write and publish my book. However, the real challenge was reaching people with my book. The real work truly began when I thought it was over. I learned that just when I thought I was done digging, that was only the warm up.

I sought to reach many people with my book and speak to audiences who might want to purchase my book. I knew that instead of waiting for the opportunities to find me, I had to go out and find the opportunities. Instead of waiting for people to ask for my book, it was time to make them want to read my book. I knew in my heart that I had done all the digging I could. I had posted about my book on social media. I had friends and family share and promote my book. I created motivational videos that promoted my book. After all this marketing, I reached a point where I felt like I had stopped reaching people with my book. I felt as though my book goals and aspirations had transitioned to a dry valley. I knew it was time to dig a little different.

I began to work toward different opportunities to gain more public exposure. First, I had to dig toward rebranding myself. I then created my own visual press release packet with a visual resume that served as a track record of my work and service. At the time, I was a graduating senior of college, and it was our celebration senior week. We had a week long list of social events to commemorate our academic achievement as graduates. However, I decided not to attend any of the events. I was not focused on celebrating past accomplishments. Instead, I was determined to work toward new ones.

Sometimes digging for our dreams and visions requires focus, isolation, and most importantly sacrifice. Sometimes in order to get what we want, we have to be willing to do things that others won't do. We have to be willing to sacrifice what others are not willing to sacrifice. We have to be willing to give up what most may not be willing to give up. That's what separates the good from those who are great and the cream from the rest of the crop. Therefore, I spent many long hours working on my press release packet. After I finished my press release packet, I set up an official email signature and changed my email picture to a professional head shot of myself.

After rebranding myself, I knew it was time to dig for the opportunities. I had no intentions of settling for what was mediocre. Instead, I set my sights on what was great. I knew I had a story, one that was meant to be told. I had every intention of my story stretching beyond those around me. I corresponded with media, television networks, and radio stations. However, I felt as though even after all my hard work, I had reached another dry valley. The media stations I contacted did not respond. I felt a bit defeated and discouraged. I was tempted to believe that maybe my book wasn't meant to reach people. That maybe I was only meant to dream small and not big.

Although I felt discouraged, I remained relentless and decided to keep digging. I continued to contact media stations. After a few weeks of not getting any responses, I woke up and realized I had an email. A local television show had invited me to speak about my book on their live broadcast. This would be my first television broadcast interview for my book. I fell to the floor in tears. I was so grateful for the opportunity. I felt as if God was honoring my digging efforts and sent this blessing to honor my hard work. But my moment of celebration was short lived. I knew it was time to prepare like never before. This was not the time to hesitate or flinch. I did not want to be good, I wanted to be great. I did not want to blend in, I wanted to stand out. This was an opportunity that should not be taken lightly. In approaching this interview, I made sure to prep myself. I even had my mother and father ask me interview-style questions to help me prepare. After prepping with my parents, I spent time practicing independently and answering questions to the wall in my room. I then memorized direct quotes and passages from my book that I was ready to recite. I approached this interview grateful, excited, and ready.

On the day of the interview, I was anxious, yet ready. The television broadcast staff put me in a room with all of the other guests for that evening. I was the youngest guest. While seated in the waiting area, one of the guests began to question me. She asked if I had a business card and website. At the time, I did not have either. In fact, all I had was a booking email. She gave me some constructive criticism, telling me that since I was about to speak on TV, I should have already been prepared with both. I realized that although God had sent the rain, I had many more holes left to dig in regards to developing my professional resume. Although I did not have the business cards or website at the time, I still had the word of God on my lips and passion that stirred deep within my soul. However, I was grateful one of the guests had taken the opportunity to plant a seed of advice within my consciousness. She could have used that opportunity to tear me down, instead she used it as a moment to build me up. She did not see me as competition but as a companion. She understood the beauty of knowing there is enough space for everyone to be great.

Right before it was my turn to interview, I stepped outside the production room to call my mother and father back home. I needed a dose of encouragement and motivation. My mother and father informed me that they and my siblings were tuned in to watch the program. This reassured me and gave me the confidence I needed. I wanted my parents to be proud of their son and for my siblings to be inspired by their brother. I wanted to perform well on this interview, not just for me but for my family. I wanted them to see themselves through me on the TV screen because their love and support played a big role in my becoming.

The Transition of Becoming

The producers escorted me on the stage when it was my turn for an interview. As I sat on the stage, I saw my book and my name on the television broadcast screen. This was one of the moments I had dreamed of and prayed for. As the production crew began to countdown, "Three…two…one…" I cracked the biggest smile at the camera and just like that I found myself on live television speaking about my book. After the interview, I felt proud and grateful for the opportunity. I felt as though I had served God's purpose and had given my best effort. By the next day, someone had ordered fifty copies of my book. This meant a lot to me. The fact that someone was inspired enough to request copies of my book in bulk gave me a sense of accomplishment. It made me feel like I was doing something right. And not only that, but I felt as though God had honored me for the holes I had dug.

If we keep digging for what it is we desire, God will send the rain. After not receiving a reply from many of the media stations, I continued to contact other media stations, and I finally received an interview on live television. Sometimes God does not drop blessings in our laps, but He holds them in our reach to see if we are bold enough to get them. Remember, you don't have to settle for being average, small, or mediocre. Whatever it is you desire, you have to be willing to dig for it. And sometimes you may not find the gold overnight, or even over time. However, you have to keep chipping away, and never stop digging. You never know how close you are to reaching your breakthrough and the blessing God has stored up for you.

I did not want the opportunities to cease with this moment. I wanted to continue to reach and inspire people with my book. I knew my only option was to keep digging once again. I continued to contact media stations. Once again, many did not reply. However, the more I dug, the more God filled my holes of opportunity. I was invited as a guest speaker on several radio stations. I was also invited to tape an interview for a television broadcast network that aired state-wide in Georgia. I was grateful for each of these opportunities. These experiences taught me that No's truly are internal, and it is up to us not to let them be external.

One of the networks that did not reply to me initially finally responded one day. They told me they were interested in my story and wanted me to do a taped interview for their television broadcast. What made this opportunity so mind-blowing was the fact that this television network was in Canada. This would be my first time speaking and traveling internationally. In preparation for the interview, my mother informed me that now would be the perfect time to have business cards made up and create a website. I obeyed her request, and created my website and business cards.

As I flew to Canada for the interview, I gazed out the window at the clouds. I reflected on the fact that just a few months ago I was traveling to my speaking engagements on a public bus. Now I had ascended to the air, and I was sailing to new heights and opportunities that had come from God. I was appreciative and said to myself, "Lord, thank you." I then felt the Lord speak to my spirit saying, "Even now, you're in the process of doing what was promised." When God said those words, I realized I should never take any moment for granted. The highs and the lows of the process is what makes the promise more bitter sweet. I did not dare take for granted what it meant to be in the air because I had so many moments on the ground. I was able to appreciate catching flights because I knew what it felt like to catch a bus. After my interview in Canada, there would be more moments when I got back on a greyhound bus to travel to my speaking engagements. However, because I knew what it felt like to be on the ground, this reminded me to never take the air for granted.

Sometimes God allows us to experience dry valleys simply because He wants us to remember the feeling so that when the rain comes we never take it for granted. When the Lord graced me with the opportunity to travel to Canada, He exceeded my expectations. I want you to know that God wants to

The Transition of Becoming

blow your mind. God wants to exceed your expectations. In fact, the Lord did just that to the Israelites. The Israelites only asked for rain. God not only told them He would send rain but also the dry valley would fill up with so much water that their army and animals would be able to drink. The Lord promised He would cause them to be victorious over the opposing army. And sure enough, this came true. Know that anytime you feel as though you have entered a dry valley, it is not by coincidence. Although, it may look hopeless, you have every reason to be hopeful because God is getting ready to send an overflow your way.

Understand, sometimes we have to prepare as we declare. Whatever we are declaring through prayer, through our journals, or even our thoughts, we have to work for it. We have to be willing to work toward what we want. Sometimes God does not meet us where we are, but He will see if we are willing to meet Him where He is. And sometimes God wants us to meet Him at the end of our hard work. Sometimes God wants us to kick down the door so that we can meet Him behind the door. Sometimes God wants us to go around the No's in our lives so that we can meet Him at the Yes's. Just remember, never stop digging. You are closer than you think. Even if it gets hard to dig, even if you have to do it alone, don't stop digging. Remember, your valley may only be dry because you are allowing it to be. Stop waiting on God because He's waiting on you. Remember in life you may receive many No's but all it takes is that one Yes for everything to change.

Just as Dory told Marlin to "just keep swimming," I am telling you to "just keep digging." Toward the end of the movie, Finding Nemo, Marlin remembered Dory's words in time of trouble. Just when Marlin was about to give up, her "just keep swimming" replayed in his head." In this moment, he did just that and he saved Nemo. I hope you remember my words in your time of discouragement just as Marlin did. Remember, "Just keep digging! Just keep digging! Just keep digging, digging, digging!"

Prayer for Perseverance

Father, I offer this prayer for perseverance in all of my life's circum-

stances. Lord help me persevere in my family life, work, and my personal endeavors. Oh Lord, help me remain persistent and consistent in my goals. Give me the strength to remain steadfast in the midst of trials and tribulations, oh God. Please help me rise above the hurdles that trip me up. Lord grant me with supernatural strength as I ask that You stretch Your hand into my life and help me lift whatever burden I am carrying. Lord walk with me in my path. When I meet resistance, help me overcome it. In times of drowning, Lord, I ask that You help me stay afloat. Lord, let Your word be my sword and Your grace be my shield, I pray this in Your all-powerful name, amen.

When was a time in your life when you felt as though you experienced a dry valley? Write about a time when you had to dig for the blessings and opportunities you prayed for. What were the opportunities and blessings you desired? Were you tempted to stop digging? How do you plan to use what was discussed in this chapter as a reminder to keep digging for what you desire?

_____

_____

_____

_____

_____

. . .

The Transition of Becoming

16

The Transition of: Promise Keeping
LETTER TO FUTURE SELF

A promise is a declaration or assurance that one will do a particular thing or that a particular thing will happen[1].

Dear future me, someday when you read this letter may you never forget the moment we wrote it. For this letter was written not after we made it to the mountain top but while walking in our path toward it. I hope you read this and believe me. If this letter has found you, then we are right where we are supposed to be. I hope that when you look back at this point in our life, you realize every transition was worth it and served its own purpose in our becoming. Remember the highs and the lows. The smiles and the tears. Know that I am fighting and pressing through each transition now so that we can become later. Right now, it may be challenging to sometimes see it, but one day when you reach the mountain top, you will be able to gaze over the horizon perplexed and in awe of how every transition was a piece to the puzzle of our becoming.

This letter shall serve both as an inspirational reminder and a daily form of accountability. When I wrote this letter, it served as a promise for us. A promise to not break the promise we made to become everything God set us out to be. The promise that no matter how hard, challenging, or frustrating it gets, and even though we may fret, we won't falter. That although we have had times when we wanted to give in, we promised we would never give up. Never forget the hopes, dreams, and promise we made in the silence of our own thoughts and through the power of our prayers. Never forget how we have defied the laws of nature through the lens of our imagination as we escaped to an alternate reality of our dreams. Promise me that what we envisioned will no longer camp in our imagination but will make itself a home in our reality.

I have prayed for you my whole life. I pray that you fight the good fight and finish the race. There will be days when we will feel so lonely and alone that we'll want to throw in the towel. There will be many reasons to turn back and abort our journey, but we must remember there are also many reasons why we must stay the course. Sometimes quitting may creep into our thoughts but know quitting is not an option. There's no quitting our becoming because so much more is on the line. Understand, we must endure so that others can know that to endure is not to suffer but to simply experience. That to be stretched does not mean to be pulled, it simply means to grow. Therefore, you need me just as much as I need you because the purpose at hand needs us both. The experiences of your past and the hope of my future must presently agree. Right now, you need me to endure so that we can testify later. You need me to write the story now so we can one day tell it. You need me to bookmark every transition now so we can one day reference these pages as a testimonial for others to believe.

May you never forget what each transition in this chapter of your becoming has taught us. Remember the letter we wrote to our younger self. The letter is to remind our younger self to let go of our menace. So also let it be a reminder for you whenever you feel as if you are battling with the menace of who we wanted to become. There will be many more times when you may feel self-condemned for not becoming a basketball player. Promise that you will continue to let go of the menace of who we once wanted to become. And this may not happen overnight for you because it is not happening overnight for me. However, promise me that we will one day be able to say we no longer contend with the menace of who we once wanted to become. May you keep the promise of never turning back from our becoming. If you are faced with another turn back moment, remember that redemption is an option. If you fall, never forget that standing back on your feet is a choice we have. Never settle for defeat or failure. Remember to take the stones of disappointment and turn them into milestones of our destiny. Remember to take what may be painful and use it as pain fuel to change the destiny of our becoming.

May you always remember to embrace our process. Embrace the highs, the lows, and the ups and downs. Embrace the moments when we will take flight and ascend to new heights, and also embrace the moments when we will operate on the ground. I know for our sake, sometimes we can let our foresight supersede our present sight. But remember to never put the cart before the horse and never try to put the promise before the process. Remember, our process is connected to our promise. And without the process there will be no promise. May you promise that you will continue to have moments when you realize our portion does have value. Remember that everything God has equipped us with regarding our dreams, aspirations, and gifts is capable of being multiplied. Remember that success is not limited to only a certain group of people. If a certain level of greatness was obtainable for someone else then success is attainable for us.

May you promise that you will remain committed to the

dream even when you have emotionally contradicting moments of being sure and then unsure. Remember that if we do not hunt the dream then the dream will haunt us. May you remember to be open to life's redirection and platform reform. Remember that sometimes change in our platform is necessary and suitable for our growth. You will be grateful for the things that did not work out how you expected. You may not see it now, but later you will. You may not understand every redirection. But sometimes we are not meant to understand, but to endure and experience. Sometimes we are not meant to know each stop God is taking us to, but sometimes we just have to sit back and enjoy the ride.

Promise that you won't let our passion move before God's pace. There will be moments when we know we are capable of running ahead and grabbing what we desire. These will be tests to see if we really trust in God's timing. Always remember our becoming is not a race, but a stride. In times of ambiguity and uncertainty, may you remember to remain patient in expectation. May you act as God's patient, trusting that He will indeed call us for our divine appointment with our destiny. May you promise to keep your heart aligned with the Lord's will. Promise me that you will not disqualify us by becoming misaligned from the lane God has for our becoming. Remember to embody the philosophy, *purpose over potential*. Just because it has the potential to be a good thing does not mean it is a God thing. Just because something has potential does not mean it is rooted in the purpose of God. As long as our heart is in alignment, we will continue to be qualified for the divine assignment the Lord has for our life.

Promise me that when the promise comes, you never forget the process. Promise me that you will attend to whatever pasture God lays before us. Promise me that the day we finally climb our way to the mountain top, never forget where we started from. Let the footprints of our pasture lead to the palace of others. Let the footprints of where we started lead others to the top. May you remember to embrace the pressing moments in our becoming.

There will always be moments when we will feel pressed. Just remember that the pressure is meant to produce something out of us. So, promise me you won't let pressing times burst our confidence and vision. Instead, promise me that you will let the pressing times extract something from us that I have yet to discover. The pressing times ahead will allow you to extract new capabilities I am currently unaware that we possess. May we promise to appreciate the moments when we feel like we have transitioned to a dark room. Promise me you will see every dark room not as God's rejection but protection. Promise that any time you are in a dark room you will believe and have faith in God's timing.

May you promise that you will never stop perfecting the prophetic of our life. Continue to preach sermons and recite poems to the walls of our room. Continue to remain consistent and persistent in our independent Bible study. Never stop maturing spiritually, academically, and Biblically. Promise that you will never stop perfecting our prophetic in private because soon we will perform in public. Promise me that you will remain multipurposed in what the Lord gives us. Protect our dreams and aspirations from moments of doubt and ambiguity. Promise that you will tend to any responsibility the Lord may entrust to us. Attend to the academic, work related, and ministry responsibilities that God places in front us. I guarantee, there may be times when we may ask ourselves, "Will this even be worth it?" However, know that it is all in the purpose of us soon ascending to the promise for our life. May you promise me that you will always keep digging for what we desire to be and aspire to achieve. If you feel yourself hanging on by a thread sometimes a thread is all you need. If we find ourselves hanging on by a piece of hope sometimes all we need is a piece. If we find ourselves experiencing a series of No's remember sometimes one Yes is all we need. Regardless of how dry the season may seem, just promise that you will never stop digging.

The Transition of Becoming

Remember, we never stop becoming. We are constantly becoming through every new transition, experience, and path we take. Even after you reach the mountain top know that behind it lies another mountain top that leads to another path of transitions. Although we may not have reached the mountain top in this chapter of our becoming, promise me you will continue to stride toward the transitions that are ahead. And when we finally reach the mountain top, promise that you won't settle for one mountain top, but you will continue down other paths of transitions in order to climb other mountains of our destiny.

Lastly, may you keep the promises that we wrote in this letter. Understand, we will one day become because I am in the transition of becoming. Therefore, I want to thank you for existing in my mind as I hope each of our experiences and transitions will one day be a memory in yours. And the day we finally reach the mountain top, we'll finally be able to look back and appreciate the path we took to get there. May we meet again at the next transition of our becoming.

Hebrews 10:36 |NIV| *"You need to persevere so that when you have done the will of God, you will receive what he has promised."*

I encourage you to write a letter to your future self. What promises do you want your future self to keep? What is something you need to tell your future self to make sure you do not give up? What can you tell yourself that will help get you through your current transitions? What in this book helped you to understand your becoming?

. . .

WARREN HAWKINS III

Recommended Reads

SHAPED FOR GREATER WORKS

"YET YOU, LORD, ARE OUR FATHER. WE ARE ALL THE WORK OF YOUR HAND."
ISAIAH 64:8

"In everything we do and every experience we have, we are being shaped by the hand of God."

WARREN HAWKINS III

About the Author

Minister Warren Hawkins III is also the author of the book *Shaped for Greater Works* and has reached millions of people with his ministry, community advocacy, leadership positions, videos on social media, national and international speaking platforms, and radio and television appearances where he inspires people of all ages and backgrounds to discover and fulfill their predestined greater works. Warren now publishes his second book *The Transition of Becoming* at twenty-three years old, as a graduating Master's college student of Clark Atlanta University.

www.warrenhawkins911.com

facebook.com/WarrenHawkinsIII
twitter.com/tattheanswerr
instagram.com/tattheanswer

Notes

The Explanation

1. "Transition." *Mirriam-Webster.com*. 2020. https://www.merriam-webster.com/dictionary/transition. Retrieval December 11, 2019.

1. The Transition of: A Menace to Minister

1. "Menace." *Mirriam-Webster.com*. 2020. https://www.merriam-webster.com/dictionary/menace. Retrieval December 12, 2019.

2. The Transition of: Redemption

1. "Redemption." *Mirriam-Webster.com*. 2020. https://www.merriam-webster.com/dictionary/redemption. Retrieval December 12, 2019.

3. The Transition of: Embracing

1. "Embrace." *Mirriam-Webster.com*. 2020. https://www.merriam-webster.com/dictionary/transition. Retrieval December 16, 2019.

4. The Transition of: Realization

1. "Realization." *Mirriam-Webster.com*. 2020. 2020. https://www.merriam-webster.com/dictionary/realization. Retrieval December 23, 2019.

5. The Transition of: Being Sure vs Being Unsure

1. "Sure." *Mirriam-Webster.com*. 2020. https://www.merriam-webster.com/dictionary/sure.
   "Unsure." *Mirriam-Webster.com*. 2020. https://www.merriam-webster.com/dictionary/unsure. Retrieval December 24, 2019.

Notes

6. The Transition of: Redirection

1. "Redirection." *Mirriam-Webster.com*. 2020. https://www.merriam-webster.com/dictionary/redirection.
   "Reform." *Mirriam-Webster.com*. 2020. https://www.merriam-webster.com/dictionary/reform. Retrieval December 27, 2019.

7. The Transition of: Stride

1. "Stride." *Mirriam-Webster.com*. 2020. https://www.merriam-webster.com/dictionary/stride. Retrieval December 28, 2019.

8. The Transition of: Patient Expectation

1. "Patient." *Mirriam-Webster.com*. 2020. https://www.merriam-webster.com/dictionary/patient.
   "Expectation." *Mirriam-Webster.com*. 2020. https://www.merriam-webster.com/dictionary/expectation. Retrieval December 30, 2019.

9. The Transition of: Heart Alignment

1. "Alignment." *Mirriam-Webster.com*. 2020. https://www.merriam-webster.com/dictionary/alignment.
   "Qualified." *Mirriam-Webster.com*. 2020. https://www.merriam-webster.com/dictionary/qualified. Retrieval December 31, 2019.

11. The Transition of: Pressing

1. "Pressing." *Mirriam-Webster.com*. 2020. https://www.merriam-webster.com/dictionary/pressing. Retrieval January 3, 2020.

12. The Transition of: The Dark Room

1. "Anointed." *Mirriam-Webster.com*. 2020. https://www.merriam-webster.com/dictionary/annointed.
   "Appointed." *Mirriam-Webster.com*. 2020. https://www.merriam-webster.com/dictionary/appointed. Retrieval January 3, 2020.

13. The Transition of: Preparation

1. "Perfect." *Mirriam-Webster.com*. 2020. https://www.merriam-webster.com/dictionary/perfect.
   "Prophetic." *Mirriam-Webster.com*. 2020. https://www.merriam-webster.com/dictionary/prophetic. Retrieval January 6, 2020.

14. The Transition of: Multipurposed Responsibility

1. Multipurposed." *Mirriam-Webster.com*. 2020. https://www.merriam-webster.com/dictionary/multipurposed.
   "Responsibility." *Mirriam-Webster.com*. 2020. https://www.merriam-webster.com/dictionary/responsibility. Retrieval January 7, 2020.

15. The Transition of: The Dry Valley

1. "Dry valley." *Mirriam-Webster.com*. 2020. https://www.merriam-webster.com/dictionary/dry valley. Retrieval January 8, 2020.

16. The Transition of: Promise Keeping

1. "Promise." *Mirriam-Webster.com*. 2020. https://www.merriam-webster.com/dictionary/promise. Retrieval January 20, 2020.

CPSIA information can be obtained
at www.ICGtesting.com
Printed in the USA
JSHW022337120723
44664JS00001B/33